Jaya Breems

Standard Vocal Literature

Mezzo-Soprano

Edited by Richard Walters

Editions of some of the songs and arias in this collection, including historical notes and translations, were previously published in the following Hal Leonard Vocal Library titles:

English Songs: Renaissance to Baroque
Edited by Steven Stolen and Richard Walters

Roger Quilter: 55 Songs
Edited by Richard Walters

The French Song Anthology
Edited by Carol Kimball and Richard Walters

The Lieder Anthology
Edited by Virginia Saya and Richard Walters

Franz Schubert: 100 Songs
Edited by Steven Stolen and Richard Walters

Anthology of Spanish Song
Edited by Maria DiPalma and Richard Walters

Gilbert & Sullivan for Singers
Edited by Richard Walters

The Oratorio Anthology
Edited by Richard Walters

The realizations are by the editor unless noted.

D1296576

To access companion recorded accompaniments online, visit:
www.halleonard.com/mylibrary

Enter Code
7835-2042-4027-5510

Cover painting: Vincent van Gogh, *The Starry Night*, Oil on canvas, 29 x 36¼", 1889

ISBN 978-0-634-07874-3

7777 W. BLUEMOUND RD. P.O. BOX 13819 MILWAUKEE, WI 53213

Visit Hal Leonard Online at
www.halleonard.com

Preface

In a constant study of collections available for voice I noticed few which attempt a comprehensive sweep of repertoire in different languages. There are admittedly some cornerstone publications addressing diverse pre-standard or teaching literature, incidentally touching on music by major vocal composers, but these are for student singers at a remedial level. Standard Vocal Literature addresses the needs of a typical college singer who has moved beyond teaching literature, but is perhaps not yet ready for a deeper look into a particular genre of song or the work of a single composer. Of course, the singer for whom this collection is a perfect fit need not be a college student. He or she also might be an advanced high school student, or an adult studying classical voice.

The principal aim of the collection is to introduce art song in five languages. The compilation plan is as follows:

- ten songs in English, representing Renaissance and Baroque music by Dowland, Purcell and others, as well as romantic song of the late 19th and early 20th centuries by Quilter, Vaughan Williams and others

- four songs in French, with special emphasis on the songs of Fauré

- six songs in German, with a sampling of music by the greatest lieder composers: Schubert, Schumann, Brahms, Strauss

- four songs in Italian that branch out beyond the standard early Italian songs students are likely to already be studying, with the deliberate inclusion of music by Bellini to get a taste of bel canto, and Stephano Donaudy, for a broader Italian romanticism

- two songs in Spanish by principal composers

Songs have been chosen with particular voice types in mind, presented in appropriate keys. Beyond art song, the collection includes:

- two opera arias, chosen from the first pieces that most singers study

- one operetta aria by Gilbert & Sullivan

- one oratorio aria as an introduction to the field

In addition to those specific parameters, we made certain that music by Mozart appears in each volume, which many would agree is the very best instruction in beautiful singing.

Because it is so important for students to learn an artistic context for music and poetry, we have provided introductory articles for all songs, including biographical and historical information that could be a springboard for more detailed research. To complete the package, we have recorded carefully prepared piano accompaniments to aid practice, and pronunciation lessons to assist in learning songs.

Each of the 30 selections in this volume is a gem in its own right. May they be the beginning of a lifelong discovery of our great heritage of vocal art music.

Richard Walters
Editor
October, 2004

Contents

SONGS IN ENGLISH

Thomas Arne
8   When daisies pied

John Dowland
12   Come again, sweet love
14   Flow my tears
11   Weep you no more, sad fountains

Henry Purcell
20   If music be the food of love
17   Nymphs and Shepherds

Roger Quilter
28   Fair House of Joy
32   It was a lover and his lass
23   Love's Philosophy

Ralph Vaughan Williams
39   Silent Noon

SONGS IN FRENCH

Georges Bizet
44   Ouvre ton cœur [2]

Gabriel Fauré
58   Clair de lune [2]
64   Mandoline [1]

Johann-Paul Martini
52   Plaisir d'amour [2]

SONGS IN GERMAN

Johannes Brahms
72   Immer leiser wird mein Schlummer [4]

Wolfgang Amadeus Mozart
77   Als Luise die Briefe ihres
ungetreuen Liebhabers verbrannte [4]

Franz Schubert
84   An die Nachtigall [4]
81   Der Tod und das Mädchen [4]

Robert Schumann
90   Du Ring an meinem Finger [4]

Richard Strauss
87   Zueignung [3]

SONGS IN ITALIAN

Vincenzo Bellini
95   Dolente immagine di Fille mia

Stefano Donaudy
99   O del mio amato ben

Alessandro Scarlatti
108   Cara e dolce

Alessandro Stradella
104   Se nel ben sempre incostante

SONGS IN SPANISH

Manuel de Falla
114   El paño moruno

Enrique Granados
111   La maja dolorosa (número 2)

OPERA ARIAS

Wolfgang Amadeus Mozart
118   Voi che sapete
Le nozze di Figaro

Christoph Willibald Gluck
124   Che farò senza Euridice
Orfeo ed Euridice

OPERETTA ARIA

Arthur Sullivan
133   When Frederic Was a Little Lad
The Pirates of Penzance

ORATORIO ARIA

Antonio Vivaldi
136   Qui sedes ad dextram Patris
Gloria

Language Coaches:

French	[1] Nicole Chandler	[2] Bernard Zinck	**German**	[3] Johanna Moore [4] Elisabeth Witte
Italian and Latin	Martha Gerhart		**Spanish**	Emma Acevedo

Composer Index

Thomas Arne
8   When daisies pied

Vincenzo Bellini
95   Dolente immagine di Fille mia

Georges Bizet
44   Ouvre ton cœur

Johannes Brahms
72   Immer leiser wird mein Schlummer

Stefano Donaudy
99   O del mio amato ben

John Dowland
12   Come again, sweet love
14   Flow my tears
11   Weep you no more, sad fountains

Manuel de Falla
114   El paño moruno

Gabriel Fauré
58   Clair de lune
64   Mandoline

Christoph Willibald Gluck
124   Che farò senza Euridice
Orfeo ed Euridice

Enrique Granados
111   La maja dolorosa (número 2)

Johann Paul Martini
52   Plaisir d'amour

Wolfgang Amadeus Mozart
77   Als Luise die Briefe ihres
ungetreuen Liebhabers verbrannte
118   Voi che sapete
Le nozze di Figaro

Henry Purcell
20   If music be the food of love
17   Nymphs and Shepherds

Roger Quilter
28   Fair House of Joy
32   It was a lover and his lass
23   Love's Philosophy

Alessandro Scarlatti
108   Cara e dolce

Franz Schubert
84   An die Nachtigall
81   Der Tod und das Mädchen

Robert Schumann
90   Du Ring an meinem Finger

Alessandro Stradella
104   Se nel ben sempre incostante

Richard Strauss
87   Zueignung

Arthur Sullivan
133   When Frederic Was a Little Lad
The Pirates of Penzance

Ralph Vaughan Williams
39   Silent Noon

Antonio Vivaldi
136   Qui sedes ad dextram Patris
Gloria

About the Accompaniment Recordings...

Our accompaniment recordings are intended as an educational tool in learning a song. We take great care to produce excellent recordings with a pianist very experienced in accompanying singers in song literature. However, it is important that teachers and singers apply insight in the use of these recordings. There is no one ideal tempo for any song. By necessity we have chosen a tempo for recording which we believe reasonably represents each song. Each singer, working with a pianist, will find his or her own best tempo to bring a song to life in rehearsals and live performance. You may find that you need slightly slower or faster tempo. You also may find your own ideas of rubato and other slight breaks in the tempo as you create your own interpretation. Above all, do not allow yourself or your students to build a rather robotic rendition of a song as a slave to the recorded accompaniment. Remember that the purpose of art song is a personal expression reflecting something real about humanity.

About the Pronunciation Recordings...

In our recordings of French and German we have used a native speaker, which we think will be most instructive. However, it is crucial to note that the guttural pronunciation of "R" in French and German on the recordings, accurate for spoken diction, needs to be modified in classical singing to a rolled or flipped "R" in German, depending on context, and generally a flipped "R" in French. We encourage you to listen to the many available recordings of famous singers of French and German song as models in this regard.

Thomas Arne

Thomas Arne was the son of an upholsterer, coffin maker, and erstwhile Handel opera producer. He was part of a colorful and musical family. Arne was born in London on or around March 12, 1710, and baptized on May 28, 1710. As a youth, Thomas smuggled a spinet into his room and muffled the strings with a handkerchief to avoid waking the rest of the family with his secret practicing. He disguised himself as a liveryman to gain access to the gallery at the Italian Opera. Following his schooling, Arne pursued a legal career for a short time until his father discovered his musical aspirations. He was ultimately allowed to abandon law to pursue a life in music. Arne gave his sister and younger brother voice lessons, and together with his siblings presented a performance of Handel's *Acis and Galatea* at London's Haymarket Theatre in 1732. Arne played the lute and violin and was a self-taught composer. He had strong interest in the stage and had tremendous success as a composer of operas and masques. The song "Rule, Britannia" is from his masque *Alfred*, written in 1740. Other notable compositions include *Rosamond* (1733), *Dido and Aeneas* (1733), *Comus* (1738), some twenty-five books of songs, and numerous instrumental works, often featuring organ or harpsichord. In 1744 he was appointed resident composer at the Drury Lane Theatre in London and held that post until a disagreement with a performer prompted him to leave for Covent Garden in 1760. Arne received particular attention and acclaim at Drury Lane for his settings of Shakespearean texts, two of which are included in this collection. He received an honorary doctorate from Oxford in 1759, hence the often-used title of Doctor Arne. Arne also composed oratorios, though was never as successful as his contemporary, George Frideric Handel. Arne's principal gift as a composer was a sure sense of melody. He died on March 5, 1778.

When daisies pied

Most of Arne's manuscripts were destroyed by fire, particularly his theatre music. "When daisies pied" is almost certainly theatre music, probably from the late 1730s or 1740s. While there is no record of a Drury Lane production of *Love's Labour's Lost* with music by Arne during his tenure, there may have been one. Or this Shakespeare text may have been used in another production.

When daisies pied

William Shakespeare
(1564-1616)
words from *Love's Labour Lost*

Thomas Arne
(1710-1778)

second time

* optional melodic ornamentation for verse 2, by the editors
** appogiatura possible

John Dowland

Englishman John Dowland stands at the forefront of early composers of what could be loosely defined as art song, with the creation or invention of the "ayre." The ayre is a simple form where the primary interest is in the top voice. The other voices are usually written in harmonizing choral style and could have been sung in that fashion, but were preferably performed by solo voice and lute. Dowland was both a singer and lutenist and traveled widely, performing his music and learning about art and style throughout Europe. His early years were marked by a period of service in Paris, working for the English ambassador, Henry Dobham. In 1580, while in Dobham's service, Dowland converted to Roman Catholicism. He returned to England in 1584, married, and tried to gain a position in Elizabeth's court. Unsuccessful, he began a period of travel that lasted until 1609, including time in Germany and Italy. Near the end of the century, Dowland returned both to Protestantism and to England, but again was unsuccessful professionally, so he went to Denmark as court musician to Christian IV in 1598. Dowland often complained that his lack of success in England was because of his acceptance abroad. It was, however, his cosmopolitan background that made his music widely known and gave it such lasting impact. His works include three volumes of lute songs (1597-1603), a set of instrumental pavans entitled *Lachrymae,* and a collection of songs with viol and lute accompaniment, *A Pilgrim's Solace.*

The songs of Dowland demonstrate his musical prowess. Early songs were generally strophic in form, with very memorable melodies, but restrained harmony. In later songs, Dowland ventured away from strophic form, choosing to through-compose to better illustrate the emotional content of the lyrics. His melodies echo the rhythm and meaning of speech. A higher degree of chromaticism and discord between the lute and the voice also serve to heighten the most dramatic and tragic parts of his songs. Dowland showed a true sense of poetry in his choice of texts, the authors of which are primarily unknown. It is possible that Dowland wrote some of the song texts himself. His songs certainly reflect the Shakespearean spirit of the era. "Come again, sweet love" dates from 1597. "Flow my tears" was composed in 1600. "Weep you no more, sad fountains" is from 1603.

Weep you no more, sad fountains

John Dowland
(1563-1626)

[Rather slow; expressively]

Weep _____ you no more, sad foun-tains; What need you flow so fast?
Sleep _____ is a re-con-cil-ing, A rest that Peace be - gets.

Look _____ how the snow-y moun-tains Heaven's sun doth gent-ly waste. But my sun's _____
Doth _____ not the sun rise smil-ing When fair at e'en he sets? Rest you then, _____

_____ heav'n-ly eyes View not your weep-ing, That now lies sleep-ing,
_____ rest, _ sad eyes, Melt not in weep-ing While she lies sleep-ing,

that now lies sleep-ing, Soft - ly, soft - ly, now soft - ly lies _____ sleep-ing.
while she lies sleep-ing, Soft - ly, soft - ly, now soft - ly lies _____ sleep-ing.

The repeat is within each of the two verses.

Come again, sweet love

John Dowland
(1563-1626)

* Small size notes are optional for verse two.

Flow my tears

John Dowland
(1563-1626)

Henry Purcell

From the time of John Dowland to the notable figures of the 20th century, Henry Purcell stands alone as the greatest British composer, and his death in 1695 marked the end of any important musical contribution from an English-born composer for nearly 200 years. Like many of his contemporaries, he came from a musical family, which included his brother Daniel, an important composer of the period as well. Henry was a chorister at the Chapel Royal at the age of 10. In 1673 he left this position and began his study with John Blow, succeeding him in 1679 as organist at Westminster Abbey. In these first years at the Abbey, Purcell began composing in earnest and wrote his first music for a play, Nathanial Lee's *Theodosius*. He went on to write music and songs for over 50 dramatic works. *Dido and Aeneas* (1689) was written for a production at a girl's school and was his only through-composed opera. Despite its humble origins, this is the first great opera in the English language. In it Purcell invented an original style of accompanied recitative, something never before composed in English. The opera remains the only representative of the period still being performed as a regular part of the repertory today. Other operatic and semi-operatic works include *King Arthur* (1691), *The Fairy Queen* (1692), and *The Indian Queen* (1695).

Purcell's other notable appointments during his brief life include service in 1682 as a Gentleman of the Chapel Royal, where he sang bass and served as one of three organists. He also became the Royal Repairman in 1683, to oversee the new organ at Temple Church. In 1685 James II named him Royal Harpsichordist. Despite these court appointments, Purcell depended greatly on the theater for income. He also composed a large amount of church and service music, including the music for the funeral of Queen Mary in 1694. This music was performed at his own funeral just one year later. His vocal music includes the ode for St. Cecilia's Day *Hail, Bright Cecilia* (1692) and the songs in *Orpheus Britannicus*, a two-volume collection published after his death. He also wrote *Nine Fantasias* (1680), *Twelve Sonatas of Three Parts* (1683), *Musick's Handmaid* (1689) for harpsichord, and another collection published posthumously, *Lessons for the Harpsichord or Spinet, Suites No. 1-8*. Little is known about Purcell's life in the 1690s. He suffered death from illness, but the nature is not known. Purcell was buried in Westminster Abbey as an honored British citizen. Of his seven children, only two were known to survive into adulthood.

If music be the food of love (First version)

"If music be the food of love" was first published in 1692 in *The Gentleman's Journal: or The Monthly Miscellany*, a magazine published by a young Huguenot refugee, Pierre Antoine Motteux. This is the first of three versions Purcell wrote between 1692 and 1695. The opening line is Shakespeare; the remainder of the text is the work of a Suffolk gentleman, Colonel Henry Heveningham. While Purcell was writing vocal music in a primarily Italianate style during the 1690s, the first version of "If music be the food of love" is an air in traditional English style. In contrast, Purcell shows a pronounced Italian influence in his third setting of this text, written in 1695.

Nymphs and Shepherds

Restoration period theatre in England greatly valued the spoken word. English audiences had rejected opera in the 17th century. Thus, the composer's theatrical opportunity was for incidental music for masques and plays. Purcell contributed music, often just a few pieces, to over 40 such productions, *The Libertine* (1692?) being one of them. Purcell composed choruses, two trios, and two songs for the play, one of them being "Nymphs and Shepherds."

Nymphs and Shepherds

T. Shadwell
from *The Libertine*

Henry Purcell
(1659-1695)

18

now, now, now, now se - cure - ly ___ rove ___ Whilst you ex - press, whilst

you ex - press ___ your jol - li - ty.

Nymphs and Shep - herds, come ___ a - way, come a - way,

Nymphs and Shep - herds, come ___ a - way, come a - way, come, come, ___ come, come ___ a - way.

optional melodic ornamentation by the editors

If music be the food of love
(First Version)

Henry Purcell
(1659-1695)

* appoggiatura possible
** optional melodic ornamentation by the editors

Roger Quilter

Roger Quilter was a breed of composer that has rarely existed after the first decades of the 20th century: he was overwhelmingly concerned with the art song. His preoccupation with the genre spanned from his youth until near his death, more than 50 years later, resulting in roughly 140 songs in total.

Quilter was born into a wealthy family in Sussex, England. He went abroad to study composition with Ivann Knorr in Frankfurt at the Hoch Conservatory. It was here that he met lifelong close friend Percy Grainger. A public career began for Quilter with the 1901 London premiere of *Songs of the Sea*, not surprisingly the composer's choice for the designation of Opus 1. Gervase Elwes, a celebrated tenor, became interested in Quilter's songs. For him the composer wrote the song cycle *To Julia*, which Elwes premiered in 1905. The same singer gave the first performance of the *Seven Elizabethan Lyrics* in 1908. Quilter's music soon gained favor, and his songs were regularly performed, particularly in London. A good pianist, the composer often served as an accompanist in London during the first decades of the 20th century.

Due to inheritance, Quilter never had to work, leaving his time and mind free for composing, though his life was not always a happy one. His wealth was limited, and in later years he was often in debt. He was plagued by chronic poor health, which prevented military service during World War I. Quilter was a well-mannered, sophisticated gentleman, with the polish of his well-to-do social class. He suffered unstable periods, with pronounced mental illness in the years leading to his death. He never married, though he formed a few close attachments and had devoted friends and supporters.

Quilter valued graceful elegance and a love of words, both qualities that are evident in his songs and his idiomatic phrasing for the voice. The imagery in his songs reflects his boyhood countryside of southern England. He was uninterested in the more extreme and progressive artistic trends of the 20th century. In general, though there are exceptions, he showed a rather refined literary taste in poetry chosen for his songs, with an inherent nationalistic British identification. Quilter's fluid and distinctive musical style, though occasionally dramatic, is most often infused with a natural, creamy English charm, though he did not compose quickly, and labored over every detail. Most agree that his best work was created rather young in his life, before his mid-40s.

Today Quilter would be considered a minor historical figure in British music overall. Regarding art song, however, very few composers working in English have matched his achievement of a living body of beloved, relevant, literate repertoire.

Fair House of Joy
from *Seven Elizabethan Lyrics*, Op. 12

Original key: D-flat Major. Composed 1907. First performance most likely by tenor Gervase Elwes and Roger Quilter, November 17, 1908, Bechstein Hall, London. Published as a set by Boosey and Co., 1908. Quilter rejected two songs originally composed for the set and wrote two new songs before the premiere. The texts for these songs had been variously published in collections. The set was dedicated to the memory of Gervase Elwes' mother, Alice Cary-Elwes, who died in 1907. The set and its individual songs have been recorded by several artists; "Weep you no more" and "Fair House of Joy" are the most often recorded, the first by Elly Ameling and others, the latter by Kathleen Ferrier and others. The composer made various arrangements of some songs of the set for voice and orchestra.

It was a lover and his lass
from *Five Shakespeare Songs*, Op. 23 (Second Set)

Original key. Three of the songs in this set were composed in 1919. "Fear no more" was composed in 1921. "It was a lover and his lass" was originally composed as a duet in 1919; the solo version was composed in 1921. Unlike the Shakespeare songs of Op. 6, which are conceptually linked, this opus is simply a collection of songs. Three of the songs were dedicated to Quilter's close friend Walter Creighton, a singer in his youth and the artist who premiered Ralph Vaughan Williams' *Songs of Travel*. The songs have been often recorded. Janet Baker was among the artists who recorded "It was a lover and his lass."

Love's Philosophy
from *Three Songs*, Op. 3

Original key: F Major. Composed c.1905. Probably first performed by tenor Gervase Elwes, to who the song is dedicated, with Quilter as pianist. Published by Boosey and Co., 1905. Published by Schott in German translation, 1924. Elwes (1866-1921) was a celebrated concert singer, and Quilter's favorite. Elwes' voice was not especially large, but was well suited to recital. He sang with clarity, finesse and sensitivity. This is one of the most recorded of Quilter's songs.

To Gervase Elwes

Love's Philosophy

from *Three Songs*, Op. 3

Percy B. Shelley
(1792-1822)

Roger Quilter
(1877-1953)

Molto allegro con moto (♩ = 112)

The foun - tains min - gle with the ri - ver And the ri - vers with the o - cean; The winds of Heav'n _____ mix for ev - er With a

To the memory of my friend, Mrs. Cary-Elwes

Fair House of Joy

from *Seven Elizabethan Songs,* Op. 12

Anonymous

Roger Quilter
(1877-1953)

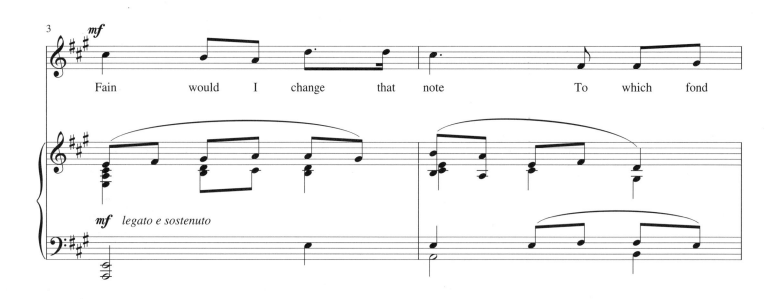

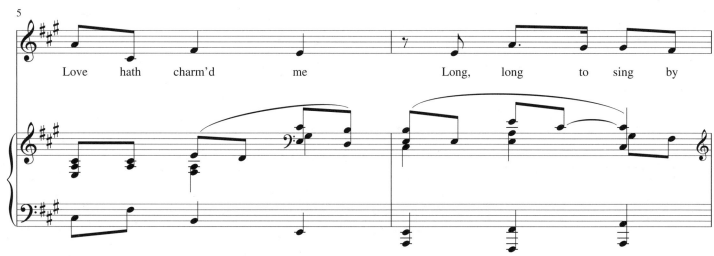

To Walter Creighton

It was a lover and his lass
from *Five Shakespeare Songs*, Op. 23 (Second Set)

William Shakespeare
(1563-1616)
from *As You Like It*

Roger Quilter
(1877-1953)

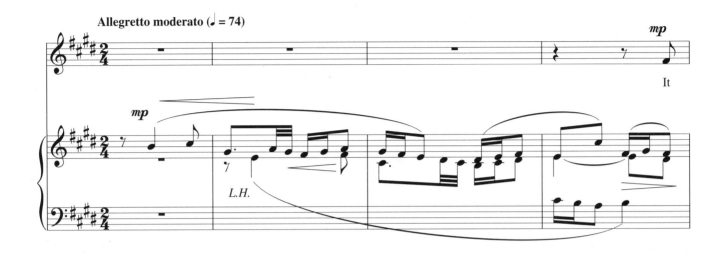

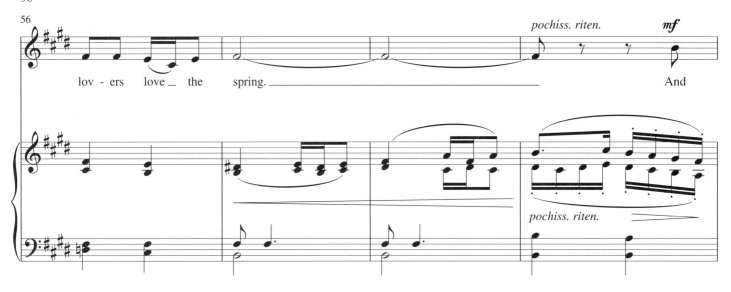

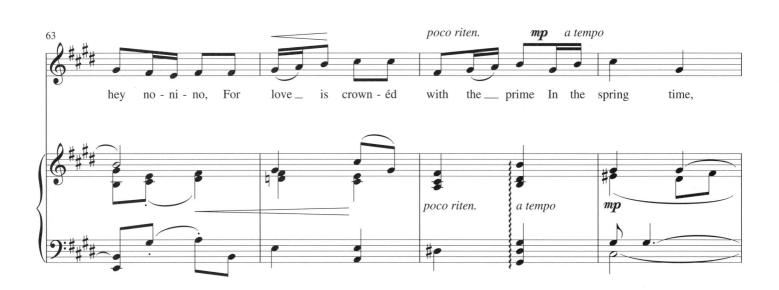

the on - ly pret - ty ring time, When

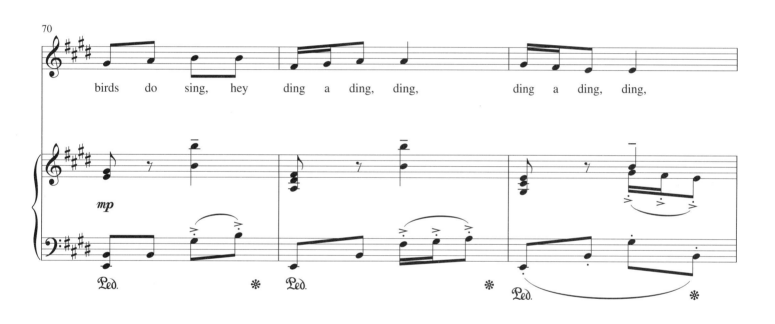

birds do sing, hey ding a ding, ding, ding a ding, ding,

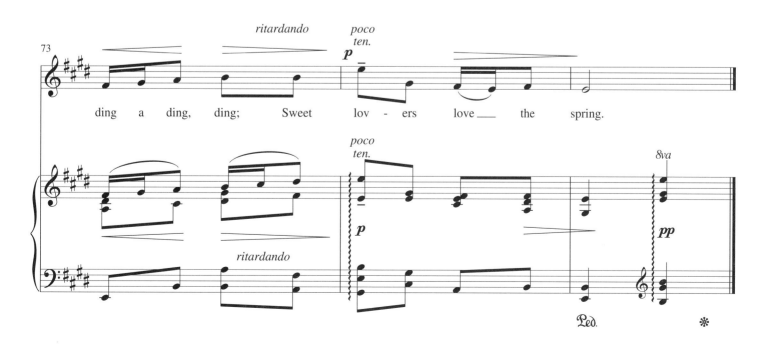

ding a ding, ding; Sweet lov - ers love the spring.

Ralph Vaughan Williams

Ralph Vaughan Williams was a major musical presence in 20th century England, working as a composer, teacher, writer, and conductor. His research into and collection of folk music and its subsequent synthesis into his compositions made Vaughan Williams a key figure in the revival of English music. His work influenced composers in England both during and after his lifetime.

Vaughan Williams was born to a distinguished family in Gloucestershire on October 12, 1872. He was related (by way of his maternal grandfather) to Charles Darwin. Ralph was encouraged as a youth to study music, taking piano and theory with one of his aunts. He would go on to study music at the Royal College of Music in London and at Trinity College in Cambridge. His primary composition teachers at this time included C. Hubert Parry, Charles Wood, and Charles Villiers Stanford. His dissatisfaction with the musical climate of England at the turn of the century led him to study composition abroad with Max Bruch (in 1897) and later with Maurice Ravel (in 1908). While these continental experiences undoubtedly influenced Vaughan Williams, he felt that the salvation of English music would not come from imitating the music of mainland Europe, but rather from the native music of England. Vaughan Williams began collecting folksongs across England in 1903, eventually amassing over 800 songs and variants. The incorporation of this folk music style into his own compositions gave Vaughan Williams' music its distinct voice, and it influenced and inspired many British composers after him. Vaughan Williams worked extensively as a conductor, often of his own works, but also leading the Leith Hill Music Festival, the Bach Choir and the Handel Society. He taught composition at the Royal College of Music, where two of his notable pupils were Gordon Jacob and Elizabeth Maconchy. His compositional output spanned nearly every genre, including operas, orchestral works (including nine symphonies), multitudes of choral works, hymns, chamber works, incidental music for plays, film scores, and a large body of songs. Vaughan Williams died on August 26, 1958, and is buried in Westminster Abbey near the burial places of his teacher Charles Villiers Stanford and Henry Purcell.

Vaughan Williams composed over 150 art songs for solo voice and piano. His first surviving song dates from 1891 and he continued to compose songs until just before his death with the *Four Last Songs* (1954-1958). Later works include *On Wenlock Edge*, a song cycle for tenor, string quartet, and piano that shows the influence of English folk music as well as his study with Ravel in Paris. The pronunciation "raif" of his first name is a misplaced pretension; the more common pronunciation is accurate.

Silent Noon

Among the best loved of Vaughan Williams songs, "Silent Noon" is from the 1903 song cycle, *The House of Life*, settings of poetry by Dante Gabriel Rossetti.

Silent Noon

Dante Gabriel Rossetti
(1828-1882)

Ralph Vaughan Williams
(1872-1958)

Your hands lie o-pen in the long fresh grass, The fin-ger- points look through like ros - y blooms: Your eyes smile peace. The pas-ture gleams and glooms 'Neath bil - low-ing

cow - pars - ley skirts ____ the haw - thorn hedge.

'Tis vis - i - ble si - lence, still _____ as the hour - glass. ____

Quasi Recitative

Deep in the sun-searched growths the drag - on - fly _____ Hangs ____

like a blue thread loos - ened from the sky:

So _____ this winged

Tempo I

hour is dropt to us from a -

bove. _____

poco rall.

Ouvre ton cœur

Louis Delâtre
(1815-1893)

Georges Bizet
(1838-1875)

Composed 1859/60. Published by Choudens, volume 2. Bizet was a natural talent, a composer in many genres, and a fantastic pianist whom Liszt once called one the three finest in Europe. He excelled in his musical education, taught by such teachers as Pierre-Joseph Zimmerman and Charles Gounoud. *Ouvre ton cœur* began life as part of a dramatic piece Bizet composed as a student in Rome, the ode-symphony *Vasco de Gama* (1859/60). The work, a composite of opera, oratorio, and symphony, is hardly known today. "Ourvre ton cœur" was published separately and posthumously. It features the bolero rhythm that Bizet was so fond of, and has become a favorite of singers who respond happily to its vocal energy and color. As in "Guitare," this song, with its evocation of Spanish music, also looks forward towards Bizet's opera *Carmen*, especially the "Chanson Bohèmienne" which opens Act 2. Bizet saw his masterpiece *Carmen* open in 1875, but died before its subsequent critical success.

Ouvre ton cœur	*Open your heart*
La marguerite a fermé sa corolle,	*The daisy closed its flowery crown,*
L'ombre a fermé les yeux du jour.	*Twilight has closed the eyes of day,*
Belle, me tiendras-tu parole?	*My lovely beauty, will you keep your word?*
Ouvre ton cœur à mon amour.	*Open your heart to my love.*
Ouvre ton cœur, ô jeune ange, à ma flamme,	*Open your heart to my desire, young angel*
Qu'en rêve charme ton sommeil.	*May a dream charm your slumber*
Je veux reprendre mon âme,	*I want to take back my soul*
Comme une fleur s'ouvre au soleil!	*As a flower opens to the sun!*

Plaisir d'amour

Jean-Pierre Claris de Florian
(1755-1794)

Johann-Paul Martini
(1741-1816)

This *romance* was composed in 1784 in Nancy, and published the following year as a supplement to the novella *Célestine*. Martini was a German composer who moved to France in 1760 and spent most of his career there. He eventually became well-known for writing opera. He is cited as the first composer in France to compose songs with piano accompaniment rather than continuo. He is most remembered for "Plaisir d'amour," a classic *romance* that remains a famous prototype of the style. The *romance* evolved from earlier French poetic-vocal forms, notably those of the troubadours. Eighteenth-century *romances* were strophic in form, with simple melodic lines that were sung without affectation. Accompaniments were subordinate to the vocal line and there was little or no musical interaction between voice and piano. "Plaisir d'amour" is notable for its rondo form and more involved accompaniment, which features a prelude, interlude, and postlude.

Plaisir d'amour	The pleasures of love
Plaisir d'amour ne dure qu'un moment,	The pleasures of love last but a moment
Chagrin d'amour dure toute la vie.	The sorrows of love last all life through.
J'ai tout quitté pour l'ingrate Sylvie,	I have given up everything for the ungrateful Sylvia
Elle me quitte et prend un autre amant.	She left me and took another lover.
Plaisir d'amour ne dure qu'un moment,	The pleasures of love last but a moment
Chagrin d'amour dure toute la vie.	The sorrows of love last all life through.
Tant que cette eau coulera doucement	As long as this water runs gently
Vers ce ruisseau qui borde la prairie,	Towards the brook that borders the meadow,
Je t'aimerai, me répétait Sylvie.	I shall love you, Sylvia told me.
L'eau coule encor, elle a changé pourtant.	The stream still flows, but she has changed.
Plaisir d'amour ne dure qu'un moment,	The pleasures of love last but a moment
Chagrin d'amour dure toute la vie.	The sorrows of love last all life through.

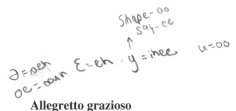

Allegretto grazioso

Clair de lune

Paul Verlaine
(1844-1896)

Gabriel Fauré
(1845-1924)

Original key: B-flat minor. Composed 1887, Op. 46, No. 32. The song was first published by Hamelle in 1888, and was orchestrated by the composer the same year. The first performance was at the Société nationale de musique, Paris, in April, 1888, sung by Marice Bagès, tenor, with orchestra. The poem is taken from Verlaine's *Fêtes galantes* (Romantic Festivities) of 1869. In these poems Verlaine blends the world of the *commedia dell'arte* (a popular comedy form improvised by traveling players, using stock characters) with the atmosphere of the *fêtes galantes* as depicted in 18th century paintings by Watteau: scenes of charming, elegantly dressed couples, amusing themselves in the great parks amidst fountains and statues. Fauré always created an atmosphere or poetic mood in his songs, nowhere more elegantly than here, an extraordinary example of text and music that mutually enhance one another. This song was Fauré's first setting of Verlaine.

Clair de lune

Votre âme est un paysage choisi
Que vont charmant masques et bergamasques
Jouant du luth et dansant et quasi
Tristes sous leurs déguisements fantasques.

Tout en charmant sur le mode mineur
L'amour vainqueur et la vie opportune,
Ils n'ont pas l'air de croire à leur bonheur
Et leur chanson se mêle au clair de lune,

Au calme clair de lune triste et beau,
Qui fait rêver les oiseaux dans les arbres
Et sangloter d'extase les jets d'eau,
Les grands jets d'eau sveltes parmi les marbres.

Moonlight

Your soul is a select landscape
That is being charmed by maskers and bergamaks.*
Playing the lute and dancing and almost
Sad under their whimsical disguises.

Although singing in a minor key
Of conquering love and seasonable life,
They do not seem to believe in their happiness
And their song mingles with the moonlight,

In the calm, sad and beautiful moonlight,
That makes the birds dream in the trees
And the fountains sob with rapture,
The big slender fountains amidst the marble statues.

*Although the term "bergamask" normally refers to a dance, Verlaine was apparently thinking of those characters of the Italian comedy, such a Harlequin, who spoke in the dialect of Bergamo.

Andantino quasi Allegretto ♩=78

The biography of the composer appears on page 70.

Mandoline

Paul Verlaine
(1844-1896)

Gabriel Fauré
(1845-1924)

Composed 1891. Op. 58, No. 1 of *Cinq mélodies de Venise*. Dedicated to Madame la princesse Edmond de Polignac. Published by Hamelle, 1891; third collections, nos. 7-11. First performance, Société nationale de musique, 2 April 1892. Florent Schmitt orchestrated "Mandoline." Fauré began composing this set in Venice, while staying at the palazzo of the Princesse Edmond de Polignac, a great patron of contemporary music and art. The Princesse was formerly Winaretta Singer, the sewing-machine heiress, who hosted one of the most elegant and influential salons in Paris. She was responsible for bringing Fauré and Verlaine together. "Mandoline," "En sourdine," and "A Clymène" are from Verlaine's collection of poems titled *Fêtes galantes*; "Green" and "C'est l'extase" come from his collection *Romances sans paroles*. Verlaine's flexible word rhythms created lyricism and fluidity in his verse, bringing back to French poetry musical qualities highly cultivated by the Renaissance poets.

Mandoline	Mandolin
Les donneurs de sérénades	*The serenaders*
Et les belles écouteuses	*And their lovely listeners,*
Échangent des propos fades	*Exchange trivial banter*
Sous les ramures chanteuses.	*Under the singing boughs.*
C'est Tircis et c'est Aminte,	*It is Tircis and Aminte,*
Et c'est l'éternel Clitandre,	*And the tiresome Clitandre,*
Et c'est Damis qui pour mainte	*And Damis, who for many a*
Cruelle fait maint vers tendre.	*Cruel woman writes many a tender verse.*
Leurs courtes vestes de soie,	*Their short silken jackets,*
Leurs longues robes à queues,	*Their long dresses with trains*
Leur élégance, leur joie	*Their elegance, their merriment,*
Et leurs molles ombres bleues,	*And their soft blue shadows,*
Tourbillonnent dans l'extase	*Whirl wildly in the rapture*
D'une lune rose et grise,	*Of a pink and gray moon,*
Et la mandoline jase	*And the mandolin chatters on*
Parmi les frissons de brise.	*Amid the shivering breeze.*

Allegretto moderato (♩ = 84)

dolce

Les don-neurs _____ de sé - ré -

p

leggiero

The biography of the composer appears on page 70.

*"fit" in previous editions of the song; "fait" is true to the original poem

ja - se Par - mi les fris - sons de bri - se.

Les don - neurs de sé - ré - na - des

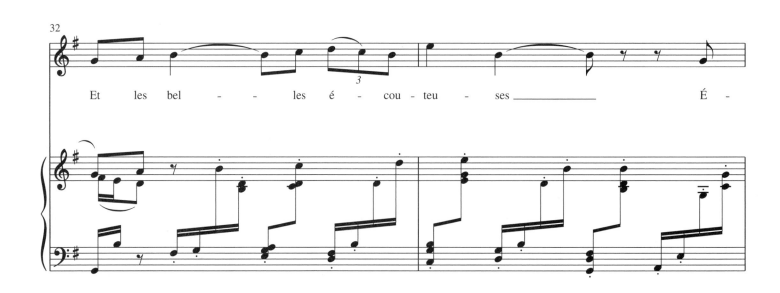

Et les bel - les é - cou - teu - ses _____ É -

chan - gent _____ des pro - pos fa - des Sous les ra -

mu - res chan - teu -

ses. _____

Gabriel Fauré

Frenchman Gabriel Fauré composed approximately 100 songs throughout his life. His first works for voice and piano date from his student days at the École Niedemeyer. At this point he was most attracted to the romantic poets, such as Victor Hugo. These early songs can be termed *romances*, and are generally strophic in form. Fauré's most important advance as a song composer with a more mature, personal style came with "Lydia," composed c.1870. In the 1880s he was drawn to the symbolists, the Parnassian poets and, most profoundly, to Paul Verlaine. The composer's song composition became bolder in the 1890s, evidenced by his cycle *La bonne chanson*. The music for voice composed in his later years, after the turn of the century (when Fauré began to suffer from deafness, probably due to arteriosclerosis), became more sparse and economical. He continued in his own highly personal compositional style, not following the dramatic changes in music brought on by Schoenberg, Stravinsky, and others, though he was well aware of their music (he was music critic for *Le Figaro* from 1903-1921), and most often admired it.

Fauré's songs were originally published in three collections of 20 songs each. (The second collection originally contained 25 songs, but upon the appearance of the third collection, recompilation occurred, putting the second collection back to 20 songs.) These collections were published by Hamelle, the first in 1879, the second in 1897, and the third in 1908. Prior to the publication of the first collection, some of Fauré's songs had been published individually, but Hamelle bought all previous rights. Fauré made very little money from his song compositions, and sold them outright for about 50 francs each for all publishing rights. The composition dates of the early songs are only approximate. His publisher asked him to retroactively assign opus numbers to the earlier songs upon their publication in the first collection of 1879. Fauré's memory was unclear about dates on many such songs. After publication he destroyed many manuscripts, so there are few clues for researchers. The tempo markings were Fauré's own, which he added at the point of publication.

Fauré worked slowly as a composer and was self-critical. He relied on the reactions of his colleagues and friends, mainly fellow composers with whom he was friendly. He admitted that at times he felt that his slow, painstaking approach to composition may have stifled spontaneity. In setting a poem, he didn't hesitate to omit verses or change words to suit his concept. Some of the small changes of words are undoubtedly oversight, but the majority were deliberate. He chose poems primarily for their pliability. Fauré said of his song composition, "seek above all to extricate the general feeling of a poem, rather than to concentrate on its details."

Harmony was Fauré's natural priority. His style was a fresh approach to tonal harmony, often freely using modes to achieve flow, fluency and ambiguity. Fauré was certainly a great melodist, but his melodies grow from the harmony, rather than standing on their own. He was somewhat of a neo-classicist in temperament, striving for a clarity of form, continuity, and craftsmanship. He valued nuance, subtlety, restraint, discretion, naturalness, sincerity, sensibility, an easy sophistication, and elegance. These aesthetic values are reflected in his writing for the voice, rarely going beyond a moderate vocal range. His songs infrequently include extroverted romantic drama. He detested verismo, sentimentality, the superficial, or anything excessive. He worried about repeating himself, but continued to be drawn to the same aesthetic approach throughout his career. It is interesting to note that although Fauré was described as a man with a lively sense of humor by those who knew him, he did not choose to write songs that were overtly witty. Because of various factors, including academic responsibilities, he composed primarily only during summer vacations throughout most of his life.

The songs were performed primarily by the composer's friends and patrons, most often in salons and in performances of the *Societé nationale de musique*. This was a close-knit circle of composers and musicians founded in 1871 by Saint-Saëns, Romain Bussine, Franck, D'Indy, Lalo, Massenet, Bizet, Guiraud, Duparc, and Fauré, with the purpose of furthering the works of the composer-members. Fauré's songs were rarely sung by celebrity singers of the time, especially before 1900. On more than one occasion he cautioned singers not to take his "slow" songs too slowly. Fauré was a good pianist, though not a virtuoso. He was admired as an interpreter of his own work, and loved to accompany his songs throughout his life, even after he was completely deaf. As a pianist, he was described as having powerful hands, a quiet nature at the keyboard, and a clarity of style that was out of fashion with the more dramatic and romantic piano performance style of his time.

Celebrity came late for Fauré. His output, including music in all genres, was known only to a small circle of Parisian society prior to about 1895. At about the age of 50 he began to be recognized more widely in France as a major musical figure. Even at his death he was virtually unknown outside France. His music includes work of consistently high quality for orchestra, for chamber ensembles, and choral works (including the well-known *Requiem*). His opera *Pénélope* is certainly a masterwork, though neglected. Without question is his unqualified place as the quintessential master of French art song. Most would agree that there is no other composer in France's history who more eloquently captured her Gallic voice in song.

Johannes Brahms

The great German composer Johannes Brahms, master of all genres of concert and recital literature, composed 196 songs for solo voice and piano, with an additional 10 songs adapted for the medium. His lieder span his entire compositional career, from about the age of 18 until his last songs of 1896, though there are years of inactivity. Additionally, Brahms made settings for voice and piano of over 200 German folksongs, most of which were unpublished in his lifetime.

Though Brahms' mentor, Robert Schumann, was himself a master lieder composer, Schubert was Brahms' closest aesthetic predecessor. Both approached composition not as a musico-poetic aesthetic, where poetry is intimately expressed in great detail in music (as was the case with Schumann or Wolf), but more as a compositional reaction to the general emotional mood and content of the poem. Brahms valued music above poetry, and melody over clearly declaimed text. The piano plays an equal but independent role in many of his songs. The musical form of each individual piece had to be perfectly satisfying to him, even if it meant altering the words in some way to suit his design. This way of working made the more dramatic, narrative form of the song cycle (not to mention opera) foreign to his creative temperament.

Brahms' advice to an aspiring song composer was to "make sure that together with your melody you compose a strong, independent bass line." Indeed, an account of Brahms reviewing a young lieder composer's work has him covering all but the vocal line and the bass line with his hands, saying that he could the judge the quality of any song in this manner. Observers noted how prominently Brahms played bass lines of his songs in accompanying singers, reflecting his natural love of counterpoint as a compositional value.

A higher percentage of Brahms' songs were written for a male singer than a female. Brahms went on recital tours as accompanist with his good friend Julius Stockhausen, and wrote many of his greatest songs for this singer. But it is clear that Brahms certainly loved the female voice, since he fell in love with at least four women singers. Many of his songs are on the subject of love. At different times in his life Brahms expressed in his songs the unrequited emotions of his complex relationships with Agathe von Siebold, Elizabeth von Herzogenberg, Rosa Girzick, Hermine Spies, and especially Clara Schumann. On the other hand, most of lyric poetry is about love, so a song composer's work is usually preoccupied with this topic. Nature figures strongly in Brahms' songs. Most characteristic is the nostalgic melancholy and loneliness that seems to permeate so much of his work, especially after his father's death in 1872.

Approximately a quarter of Brahms songs are in simple strophic form. Another quarter are through-composed. Most of the rest are in the form he perfected, something one can term as the varied strophic. Subsequent verses may contain variations in any number of ways to accommodate the subject and character of the progressing poem. "Wie Melodien zieht es mir" and "Vergebliches Ständchen" are examples of varied strophic songs. Sometimes a middle verse will be composed to new music, and the final verse will be a variation on the first, resulting in an ABA form that is still related to the varied strophic, as in the Kugler song "Ständchen."

The compositional dates for Brahms' songs are oftentimes difficult to pin down, for he habitually started something that was not completed in final form for several years. Of song composition he instructed, "Let it rest, let it rest, and keep going back to it until it is completed as a finished work of art, until there is not a note too many or too few, not a bar you can improve on."

Immer leiser wird mein Schlummer

Hermann von Lingg
(1820-1905)

Johannes Brahms
(1833-1897)

Original key. "The poem of the dying girl by H. Lingg and your setting of it thrilled me…I am not ashamed to confess that I could not finish playing it for my tears." So wrote Brahms's friend Theodor Billroth after receiving this song, Op. 105, No. 2. The work was composed in 1886 and published in 1889 by N. Simrock. The author Lingg wrote large-scale dramas and epics, but it was for his short poems that he was best known. This was published in his *Gedichte* of 1855.

Immer leiser wird mein Schlummer

Immer leiser wird mein Schlummer,
Nur wie Schleier liegt mein Kummer,
Zitternd über mir.
Oft im Traume hör ich dich
Rufen draus von meiner Tür,
Niemand wacht und öffnet dir,
Ich erwach und weine bitterlich.

Ja, ich werde sterben müssen,
Eine andre wirst du küssen,
Wenn ich bleich und kalt.
Eh die Maienlüfte wehn,
Ehn die Drossel singt im Wald:
Willst du mich noch einmal sehn,
Komm, o komme bald!

Ever lighter becomes my slumber

Ever lighter becomes my slumber;
like a veil lies my sorrow,
trembling over me.
Often in my dreams I hear you
calling outside my door.
No one wakes and opens for you;
I wake up and weep bitterly.

Yes, I shall have to die;
you will kiss another
when I am pale and cold.
Before the May breezes blow,
before the thrush sings in the wood,
if you want to see me once more,
come – o come soon!

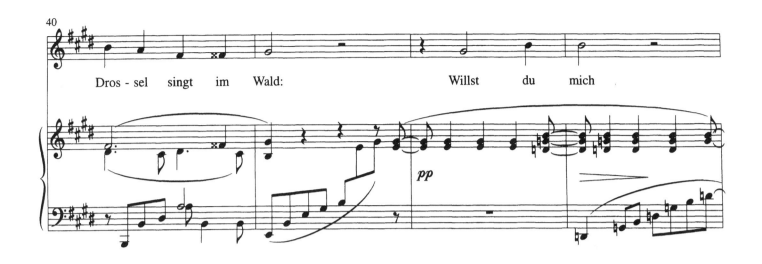

Dros - sel singt im Wald: Willst du mich

noch ein - mal sehn, komm, o kom - me

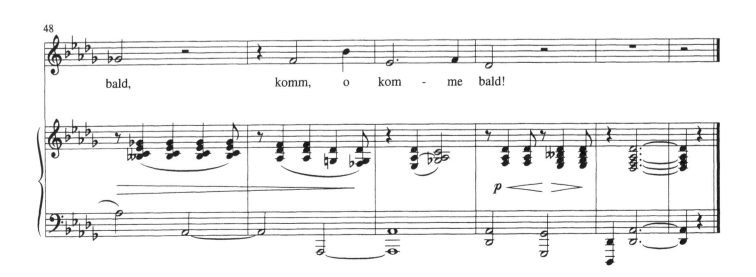

bald, komm, o kom - me bald!

Wolfgang Amadeus Mozart

The great Wolfgang Amadeus Mozart was a master of any form he chose, including the occasional solo song. The art song was not a developed genre during his lifetime. Mozart's songs number only about 30 among an enormous output of operas, symphonies, choral works and chamber music. The lieder movement of 19th-century Germany and Austria, which championed romantic ideals in its personal poetry by masters such as Goethe, Rückert, and Heine, had not taken hold yet during Mozart's lifetime. By the mid-18th century, vocal music accompaniments had evolved from being realized at sight from figured bass by a performer to being fully written out by a composer. Later in that century songs were usually written by minor composers, and almost always strophic in form, with the voice line often in an uninspired, serviceable melody, closely mirrored in the piano accompaniment. Prior to Mozart's work, few songs treated the voice and piano independently and equally.

The pianoforte of Mozart's day was a new instrument, just beginning to provide the dynamic and emotional range necessary to play a concerto with orchestra, or to adequately accompany an expressive vocal or chamber performance. The rise in popularity of the piano in the decades after Mozart's death contributed to a culture ready for salon concerts perfect for lieder.

Mozart's songs were generally intended for home entertainment. They were not commissioned, but composed as gifts for hosts, friends or colleagues, or as romantic gestures. There were many singers in Mozart's circle of friends and family, including his wife and sister-in-law. His understanding of the voice as an instrument comes through in music written for those voices he knew best. Though there was little, if any, money to be made from songs in his time, Mozart still continued planning such compositions at various times throughout his life, though he viewed them as incidental pieces. Even the very existence of Mozart's songs reveals his love for the voice and piano.

The texts Mozart used for his songs were often casually chosen, written by friends or lesser-known poets. Mozart composed songs primarily to German words, with an occasional Italian or French text. Except for one setting of Goethe ("Das Veilchen"), he did not seek out high literature to set to music. Mozart's compositional style, with a strong sense of musical form, instead gravitated to simpler texts that could be molded to his musical design. The composer's often quoted philosophy about word-setting was stated in a letter to his father about the libretto for *Die Entführung aus dem Serail*: "…the poetry must be altogether the obedient daughter of the music…when music reigns supreme and one listens to it, all else is forgotten."

Most of Mozart's earliest songs were simple strophic works in the tradition of folksongs. Occasionally a simple arietta reminiscent of an opera aria was composed, such as "Ridente la calma," Mozart's only *da capo* song in Italian. Mozart's later songs were written around the same time as the Lorenzo da Ponte operas, *Le Nozze di Figaro*, *Don Giovanni*, and *Così fan tutte*. These songs are through-composed and sometimes have the same kind of accompanied recitative style that is commonly heard in these Mozart operas. Some of his works hint toward mature lieder, with an intimate union of poetry and music, such as "Abendempfindung."

Despite the minor place song plays in Mozart's work, every piece he created bears the exquisite taste, natural craft and elegance of a master composer. The songs are also fascinating as a distilled concept of vocal melody by one of the greatest of melodists.

Als Luise die Briefe ihres ungetreuen Liebhabers verbrannte

Original key. K. 520. Once misattributed to Mozart's friend and student Gottfried von Jacquin, Mozart completed this song on May 26, 1787, written while visiting Jacquin. It was published in Vienna in 1789; Jacquin provided the dedication to "Fräulein von Altomonte.". Katherina von Altomonte would later be one of the soloists in the 1789 premiere of Mozart's reorchestrated version of Handel's *Messiah*. This dramatic scene of the abandoned Luise reflects the style of accompanied recitative commonly heard in Mozart's operas, such as *Don Giovanni*, which was composed in the same year. Baumberg, a Viennese poetess, said that she wrote the text from a similar experience of her own.

Als Luise sie Briefe ihres ungetreuen Liebhabers verbrannte	*As Louise Burned Her Faithless Lover's Letters*
Erzeugt von heißer Phantasie, In einer schwärmerischen Stunde Zur Welt gebrachte, geht zu Grunde! Ihr Kinder der Melancholie!	*Made by burning fantasy, in a rapturous hour into the world brought, go back to dust, you children of melancholy!*
Ihr danket Flammen euer Sein: Ich geb' euch nun den Flammen wiede, Und all die schwärmerischen Lieder; Denn ach! er sang nicht mir allein.	*You owe the flames your life, I give you back now to the flames, and all the rapturous songs, because ah! he sang them not for me alone.*
Ihr brennet nun, und bald, ihr Lieben, Ist keine Spur von euch mehr hier: Doch ach! der Mann, der euch geschrieben, Brennt lange noch vielleicht in mir.	*You burn now, and soon, you loved ones, is no more trace of you here. But alas! the man, who had written you, shall perhaps burn a long time within me.*

Als Luise die Briefe ihres ungetreuen Liebhabers verbrannte

Gabriele von Baumberg
(1768-1839)

Wolfgang Amadeus Mozart
(1756-1791)

Er - zeugt von _ hei - ßer Phan - ta - sie, in ei - ner

schwär - me - ri - schen Stun - de zur Welt ge - brach - te, geht zu Grun - de! geht zu

Grun - de! ihr __ Kin - der __ der Me - lan - cho - lie!

Ihr dan - ket Flam - men eu - er

Franz Schubert

The talents of Franz Schubert are well chronicled in any music history source. His nine symphonies, choral pieces, and countless piano and chamber works make him, of course, a major European musical figure, particularly as a transitory talent from the Classical to the Romantic. It is, however, his work as a song composer, producing over 600 lieder, which insures him a unique place in history. His song composition began at least as early as age 14 and continued until his death, with some periods of enormous output. In the two year period of 1815 and 1816 he wrote a remarkable 250 songs.

Schubert reinvented the lied, going much further in the endeavor of setting poetry to music than anyone before him. He created the first substantial body of literature for the vocal recital. His accomplishment, however great, could not have happened without the rise of German lyric poetry by Johann Wolfgang von Goethe, Heinrich Heine, Wilhelm Müller, Ludwig Rellstab, Friedrich Rückert, and Johann Christoph Friedrich von Schiller during the late 18th century and first decades of the 19th century. Schubert also set texts by many minor literary figures, some of which were friends.

Musical success during Schubert's lifetime was measured against Beethoven in the concert hall and Rossini in the opera house. Schubert dreamed of triumph in both places, but never achieved it, almost always failing to find performances of his larger works. As an alternative, the devoted circle of friends around the composer would gather in living rooms and parlors for evenings which came to be called Schubertiads. A majority of the songs were first performed there. These evenings encouraged Schubert in song composition, since there was a ready place, performers and audience for the works. The composer was at the piano regularly in the Schubertiads, accompanying songs and playing piano pieces, but never performed for a wider public. His piano abilities seem to have been adequate but not remarkable. Schubert had many favorite singers, lyric baritone Johann Michael Vogl and soprano Anna Milder Hauptmann among them. On occasion Schubert himself sang a new song for the intimate Schubertiad audience, though he never would have considered himself a singer.

Schubert explored various musical forms in his songs, including strophic, through-composed, freely declamatory, and combined structures. His text setting shines with a balance of sensitivity to words and strong melodic values. The piano accompaniment figures imaginatively reflect the mood and imagery of the texts. Among Schubert's achievements as a song composer is the full flowering of the concept of a narrative song cycle, a group of related poems which tell some kind of story by their progression, shown in the expansive sets *Die Winterreise* and *Die schöne Müllerin*.

Schubert's composition was inspired by many influences. He loved the operas of Gluck, and discovered the baritone Vogl at a performance of *Iphegénie en Tauride*. Schubert also greatly admired Handel, and in his free time played through that composer's operas and oratorios. He thought Mozart's *Don Giovanni* among the very best of all operas, and valued the overture to *Die Zauberflöte* as a masterwork with few peers. As for Beethoven, Schubert held him in high regard. Though they both lived in Vienna, the two never met until 1827, and then briefly, with Beethoven virtually on his deathbed. Five years earlier Schubert dedicated a set of published piano variations to Beethoven and brought a copy to him. The great and famous man was not at home, and humbled by the idea of a return visit, Schubert simply left the new edition. Beethoven apparently approved of the music, and played it nearly every day thereafter with his nephew.

Der Tod und das Mädchen

Matthias Claudius
(1740-1815)

Franz Schubert
(1797-1828)

Original key. D 531. This song was composed in February, 1817, and published in November, 1821, by Cappi and Diabelli as Opus 7, No. 3, with a dedication to Ludwig, Count Széchényi. Following Schubert's death, the autograph found its way to his step-brother, Andreas, who divided it up into eight pieces, giving one each to his favorite students. Sections of the song, notably the piano prelude and accompaniment figures, were adapted by Schubert in 1824 for the theme and variations movement of his D minor string quartet, D 810.

Matthias Claudius was a theology student, later turning to political science and law before becoming a poet (publishing under the pseudonym Asmus) and the editor of the *Wandsbecker Bote* (Wandsbeck Messenger). In later life he returned to religion as his major interest. "Der Tod und das Mädchen" has a long tradition of performances by great contraltos and mezzo-sopranos. Regarding the final vocal note of the song, it appears that both the low D and the octave higher were in the first edition, and there are manuscript sources for both. It may be assumed that the composer's intention was to sing the lower note if it is within the singer's usable range.

Der Tod und das Mädchen	*Death and the Maiden*
Das Mädchen	*The Maiden*
Vorüber, ach vorüber,	*Pass by; ah, pass by.*
Gehn wilder Knochenmann!	*Get away, wild skeleton!*
Ich bin noch jung, geh Lieber,	*I am still young. Away, dear man,*
Und rühre mich nicht an.	*and touch me not.*
Der Tod	*Death*
Gib deine Hand, du schön und zart Geibild,	*Yield your hand, you beautiful and tender creature;*
Bin Freund und komme nicht zu strafen.	*I am a friend, and come not to chastise.*
Sei gutes Muts! ich bin nicht wild,	*Be of good cheer! I am not wild;*
Sollst sanft in meinen Armen schlafen.	*you shall sleep softly in my arms.*

über, geh wil - der Kno - chen - mann! Ich bin noch

cresc.

jung, geh Lie - ber, und rüh - re mich nicht an, und

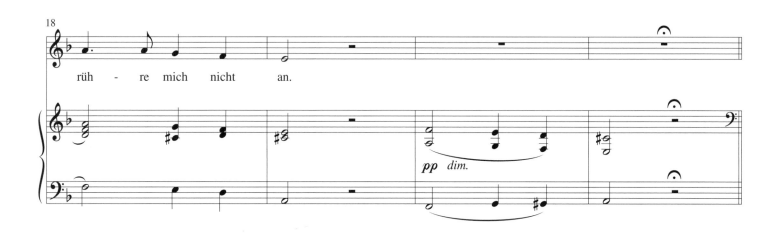

rüh - re mich nicht an.

pp dim.

Tempo primo

Der Tod:

Gib dei - ne Hand, du schön und zart Ge - bild, bin

pp

Freund und kom - me nicht zu___ stra - fen.

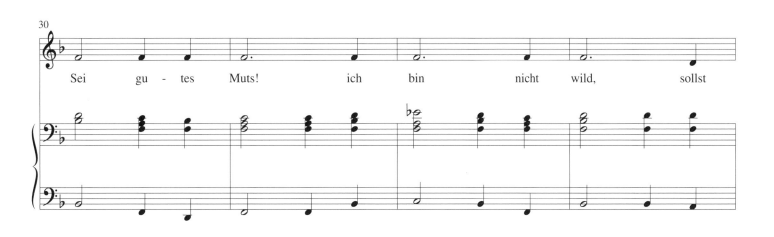

Sei gu - tes Muts! ich bin nicht wild, sollst

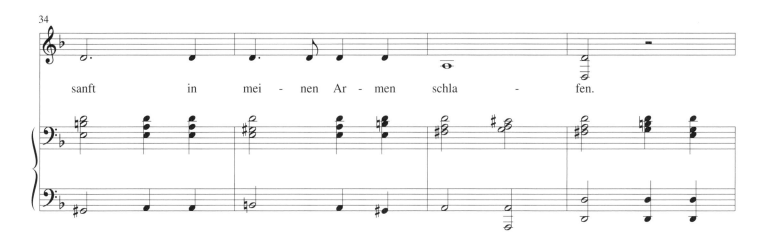

sanft in mei - nen Ar - men schla - fen.

An die Nachtigall

Matthias Claudius
(1740-1815)

Franz Schubert
(1797-1828)

Original key: G major. D 497. Schubert's song was probably composed in November, 1816. It was not published until 1829. There is a striking similarity between the songs "An die Nachtigall" and "An die Geliebte," composed 13 months earlier and possessing a nearly identical theme. Matthias Claudius was a theology student, later turning to political science and law before becoming a poet (publishing under the pseudonym Asmus) and the editor of the *Wandsbecker Bote* (Wandsbeck Messenger). In later life he returned to religion as his major interest. This poem was written in 1771, with the original title "Nachtigall, Nachtigall, ach!"

An die Nachtigal

Er liegt und schläft an meinem Herzen,
Mein guter Schuztgeist sang ihn ein;
Und ich kann fröhlich sein und scherzen,
Kann jeder Blum und jedes Blatts mich freun.
Nachtigall, ach! Nachtigall, ach!
Sing mir den Amor nicht wach!

To the Nightingale

He lies and sleeps upon my heart;
my good guardian spirit sang him to sleep.
And I can be joyful and can have fun –
can delight in every flower and every leaf.
Nightingale, ah! Nightingale, ah!
Do not sing my love awake!

Richard Strauss

Richard Strauss was a German composer and conductor who made significant contributions to many musical genres, including major compositions for the voice. He was one of the strongest musical influences of the post-Wagner Germany of the late 19th and early 20th centuries. Richard was born on June 11, 1864 in Munich, to a musical family. His father, Franz Strauss, was the principal horn player of the Munich Court Orchestra for nearly 50 years. His mother, Josephine Pschorr, was part of a family of brewers. The Strauss family enjoyed financial independence, and as a result, Richard had a carefree upbringing. He showed musical interest at a very young age. At age four he took piano lessons from August Tombo, and at age eight he took up the violin with Benno Walter, concertmaster of the Munich Court Orchestra. His musical education eventually led him to conducting and composing, assisting the famed Hans von Bülow with his orchestra in Meiningen. Strauss' fame as a composer was assured with the 1889 premiere of his tone poem *Don Juan*, a tremendous success that brought him regard as the most significant and progressive composer since Wagner. Strauss would go on to write many other tone poems including *Don Quixote, Tod und Verklärung, Ein Heldenleben, Also sprach Zarathustra*, and *Till Eulenspiegels lustige Streiche*. His recognition as a world-class conductor during his early career is equally important. Strauss appeared as a guest conductor in Holland, Spain, France, and England in 1897 alone. In 1898 he was appointed chief conductor of the Royal Court Opera in Berlin, where he conducted 71 performances of 25 operas in his first eight-month season. He also conducted Wagner at Bayreuth during his illustrious career. In addition to his work as a composer and conductor, Strauss was a tireless champion of composer's rights and he campaigned for seven years to revise German copyright law to pay royalties to composers for performance and publication of their works.

While Strauss' symphonic masterpieces brought him great recognition, it was to opera that he would primarily turn after 1898. His first opera, *Guntram*, was a failure, but Strauss followed that up with the successful *Feuersnot*. Nothing could prepare theatregoers, however, for Strauss' next project. *Salome*, with its overt sexuality and gruesome content, caused an immediate scandal at its 1905 premiere in Dresden. With the controversy came free publicity, and *Salome* was produced in 50 opera houses in the two years following its premiere. Strauss would write operas for most of the rest of his life, including *Elektra, Der Rosenkavalier, Ariadne auf Naxos, Die Frau ohne Schatten, Intermezzo, Die ägyptische Helena, Arabella, Die schweigsame Frau, Friedenstag, Daphne, Die Liebe der Danae*, and *Capriccio*. After *Elektra*, his aesthetic style retreated to a more conservative approach, where he remained the rest of his career.

Amid the large works, Strauss was also an active lieder composer for most of his career. Strauss' ability to write for the voice, strikingly apparent in his operas, is evident in his many songs. Strauss composed over 200 songs during his lifetime, the majority of which he wrote between 1885 and 1906. It is apparent that Strauss the song composer paved the way for Strauss the opera composer. A 12-year hiatus in song composition ended in 1918, and Strauss composed songs until his final work in the 1940s, though he never achieved the pace of song output as the period before 1900. In his early lieder he was undoubtedly inspired to write for the voice after meeting and eventually marrying Pauline de Ahna, a renowned German soprano. They met in 1894 when Pauline sang Elisabeth in Wagner's *Tannhäuser* with Strauss conducting at Bayreuth. Many of Strauss' songs were written with her voice in mind; Strauss gave the songs of Op. 27 to Pauline as a wedding gift. He wrote 31 songs in six collections during 1899-1901 alone.

Though Strauss was himself a competent pianist, he wrote very little literature for the instrument. The song accompaniments are our best understanding of Strauss as a composer for piano. His piano accompaniments partner equally with the voice and characterize the general mood of the text being sung. The piano accompaniments also tend to be orchestral in nature, with broad, sweeping gestures or exquisitely delicate colors. It was a logical progression then that Strauss developed the lied with orchestra further than any composer before him. He orchestrated 27 of his songs originally written for voice and piano, and composed 15 songs directly for voice and orchestra. While Strauss, a brilliant orchestrator, was naturally drawn to the orchestral lied as a genre, there was a practical reason as well. He orchestrated many of his songs specifically for concerts which he conducted with his wife Pauline as soloist during the 1890s.

Influences range from Mozart to Wagner in a style that is unmistakably Straussian. As with his operas, Strauss is able to lucidly depict characters through his songs, utilizing effective text setting and richly descriptive piano accompaniments. Strauss grew up in a musical culture heavily influenced by Wagner. Both composers shared a strong sense of harmonic tension and resolution sustained over long phrases. Strauss' lieder are more compact than the larger works, and hence less spacious in harmony and form, but they still contain the characteristic sureness of harmonic direction and arching phrases. Strauss nearly always wrote vocal music, including opera, with the lyric voice as his inspiration, as Mozart did. This contrasts with Wagner, who most often composed with larger, more dramatic voices in mind. As most of Strauss' songs were originally performed in the concert hall, they have a distinct style that differs clearly from lieder composed for the salon or other intimate venues. In general, the songs are musically conservative, rarely moving to the modern "decadence" of *Salome* and *Elektra*.

Zueignung

Hermann von Glim
(1812-1864)

Richard Strauss
(1864-1949)

Original key: C major. Poet Glim was of aristocratic birth and worked much of his career in minor government posts. He married at age forty-nine and died at fifty-one. His poetry of love and love's suffering seems perfectly suited for Strauss's Op. 10 collection, often considered the real beginning of the composer's lieder-writing career and the first group of Strauss's songs to appear in print (Joseph Aibl Verlag, 1887). Op. 10 opens with this song, a dedication. Each of the three stanzas begins with the same four measures, indicating a nearly strophic setting, but then fresh music concludes each statement. Both Heger and Strauss orchestrated the song, with Heger's version being in wider use since Strauss's includes many changes personal to the dedicatee, soprano Viorica Ursuleac.

Zueignung	Dedication
Ja, du weisst es, teure Seele,	*Yes, you know it, beloved soul,*
Dass ich fern von dir mich quäle,	*that I am tormented far from you,*
Liebe macht die Herzen krank,	*love makes the heart suffer,*
Habe Dank.	*thanks to you.*
Einst hielt ich, der Freiheit Zecher,	*Once I held, the one who delighted in freedom,*
Hoch den Amethysten-Becher,	*high the amethyst cup,*
Und du segnetest den Trank,	*and you blessed the drink,*
Habe Dank.	*thanks to you.*
Und beschworst darin die Bösen,	*And exorcised the evil ones therein,*
Bis ich, was ich nie gewesen,	*until I, as I had never been,*
Heilig, heilig an's Herz dir sank,	*holy, holy onto your heart I sank,*
Habe Dank.	*thanks to you.*

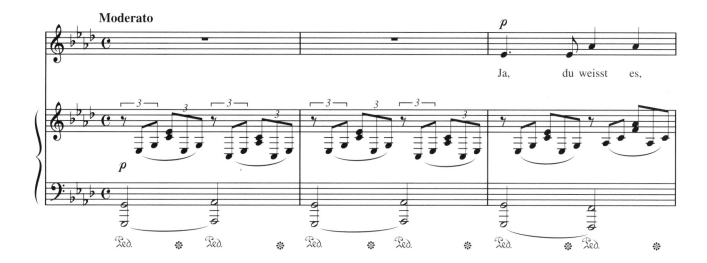

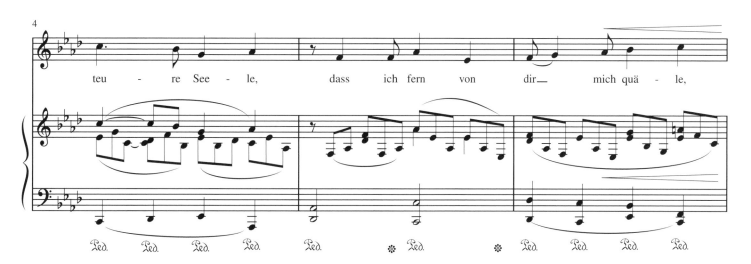

Du Ring an meinem Finger

Adalbert von Chamisso
(1781-1838)

Robert Schumann
(1810-1856)

Original key. This is the fourth song in Schumann's renowned song cycle *Frauenliebe und –leben*, composed in July of 1840 after a court decision awarded Robert Schumann and Clara Wieck the right to marry against her father's prohibition. It was published as part of the eight-song cycle by Whistling in 1843 as Op. 42, No. 4. Poet Chamisso was from a family that had to flee France due to the revolution; he settled in Berlin and was active as a botanist as well as a poet. In the cycle, Chamisso's poems follow the course of a woman's emotional life from courtship through marriage, motherhood, and widowhood. Representing the bride's tender feelings, this song holds an important and central place in the cycle. A ninth poem, in which the woman advises her granddaughter, was not set by Schumann.

Du Ring an meinem Finger

You Ring on my Finger

Du Ring an meinem Finger,
Mein goldenes Ringelein,
Ich drüke dich fromm an die Lippen,
An das Herze mein.

Ich hatt' ihn ausgeträumet,
Der Kindheit friedlich schönen Traum,
Ich fand allein mich, verloren
Im öden, unendlichen Raum.

Du Ring an meinem Finger,
Da hast du mich erst belehrt,
Hast meinem Blick erschloßen,
Des Lebens unendlichen, tiefen Wert.

Ich will ihm dienen, ihm leben,
Ihm angehören ganz,
Hin selber mich geben und finden
Verklärt mich in seinem Glanz.

You ring on my finger,
my little golden ring,
I press you devoutly to my lips,
to my heart.

I had finished dreaming
childhood's peaceful, beautiful dream;
I found myself alone and forlorn
in empty, infinite space.

You ring on my finger,
there you have first taught me,
have unlocked my eyes
to life's deep eternal worth.

I will serve him, live for him,
belong to him entirely,
give myself and find
myself transfigured in his splendor.

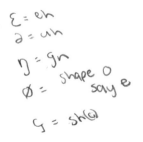

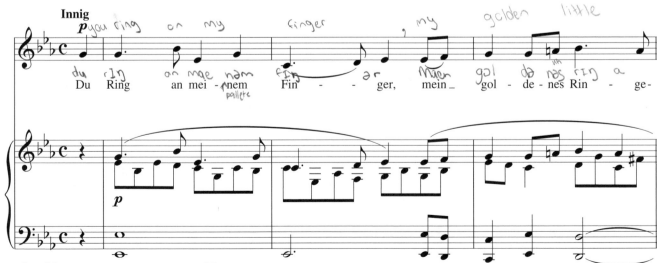

The biography of the composer appears on page 94.

Robert Schumann

Robert Schumann was one of the most significant German composers of the 19th century, creating masterpiece symphonies, piano works, chamber music, choral music, and lieder. His songs furthered the full blossoming of the German lieder aesthetic, championing romantic ideals in its deeply personal poetry by masters such as Goethe, Rückert, and Heine.

Schumann was born in Zwickau in 1810 as the youngest of five children. His father worked as a bookseller and publisher, and the young Robert did extensive reading of literature in his father's shop. After finishing his education at the Lyceum in Zwickau, Schumann began law studies at the University of Leipzig, though he apparently never attended a single class, focusing rather on his musical ambitions. In August of 1828 he began piano studies with Friedrich Wieck, making the acquaintance of his nine-year-old daughter, Clara. Schumann founded the *Neue Zeitschrift für Musik* in 1834 with Wieck and others, a periodical featuring musical critiques and other articles; he served as editor of this periodical for several years. Through the *Neue Zeitschrift*, Schumann championed the works of the young Johannes Brahms, who became a close family friend. Schumann eventually married Clara Wieck in 1840 after a lengthy legal battle with her father, who rigorously objected to the marriage. Among other things, Herr Wieck accused Schumann of being a habitual drunk. The Schumann household was a productive, busy one for a few years. Robert encouraged Clara, a great concert pianist, to compose, and in most ways theirs was a modern marriage of equality. But Schumann's life was plagued by fragile mental health. He attempted to take his own life in 1854 by throwing himself into the Rhine, but was rescued by fishermen. After the suicide attempt he was taken in at a private asylum, where he remained until his death in 1856.

For Schumann, 1840 was an important year. In addition to his long-awaited marriage to Clara, Schumann's composition turned radically to the song, a genre in which he had written only sporadically, previously considering it inferior to instrumental music. Suddenly the composer delivered "The Year of Song," with the *Liederkreis* (Op. 24 and Op. 39), *Dichterliebe* (Op. 48), and *Frauenliebe und –leben* (Op. 42). Of the over 200 songs that Schumann composed, 138 were written during 1840, often at the pace of one or more songs per day. Individual songs of note from 1840 include "Mondnacht," "Die beiden Grenadiere," and "Mit Myrthen und Rosen." Schumann also composed *Myrthen* (Op. 25) during the same year as a wedding present to Clara, a collection of 26 songs which includes "Widmung," "Die Lotosblume," "Der Nussbaum," and "Du bist wie eine Blume." He continued to write songs for the remainder of his life, though never with the same urgency or as passionately as in 1840. Clara clearly inspired this lyric output. Additionally, songs were small compositions that could be quickly sold to publishers, generating instant income for a man not only about to be married, but in the midst of proving himself worthy as a husband in court.

Schumann's most notable contribution to the development of the lied was his use of the piano as compositional equal to the voice. During his early career he devoted the majority of his efforts to writing short, characteristic piano pieces, developing the piano "miniature" to a perfectly self-contained piece, often suggesting extra-musical meanings. Schumann's ability to write miniatures for piano led naturally to his style as a song composer. His songs elevate the piano to an important role in clarifying and in many cases heightening the meaning of the text. This was also aided by the development of the pianoforte from the version Schubert knew to the more sustained and nuanced instrument of Schumann's day. The piano parts are often given melodic material that intertwines with the vocal line. He also sometimes composed lengthy piano interludes and epilogues in his songs (the latter most notably in the cycle *Dichterliebe*), a new innovation at the time.

Schumann's style as a lieder composer is undeniably romantic in nature. He exhibited excellent taste in choosing texts by German poets such as Heinrich Heine and Joseph von Eichendorff, likely a product of his early exposure to literature and poetry through his father's business. Schumann was also an active writer throughout his life, from his work as a music critic for the *Neue Zeitschrift* to the marriage diary he kept with Clara. It is not surprising then that Schumann considered words to be the equal of music in the composition of a song. While some future composers such as Hugo Wolf adopted this approach, composers such as Johannes Brahms and Richard Strauss wrote songs that ultimately place more value on musical qualities than poetic ones.

Dolente immagine di Fille mia

Giulio Genoino
(1847-1903)

Vincenzo Bellini
(1801-1835)

Original key. Vincenzo Bellini was born on November 3, 1801, in Catania, Sicily. His musical family recognized and encouraged his talents, with the young Vincenzo composing his first complete piece at the tender age of 6. Vincenzo's musical education was the responsibility of his father and grandfather. In 1819 his family sent him to the Real Collegio di Musica in Naples to complete his formal music education. It was there that Bellini's career as an opera composer was born. His opera *Adelson e Salvini* was premiered at the school in 1825, and its success led to a commission for his next opera, *Bianca e Fernando* (later renamed *Bianca e Gernando*). His collaboration with librettist Felice Romani began with the premiere of *Il pirata* at La Scala in 1827. The Bellini/Romani partnership produced six more operas, including *I Capuleti e i Montecchi*, *Norma*, and *La sonnambula*, three of Bellini's best-known works. Bellini's final opera, *I puritani*, was premiered in Paris on January 24, 1835. Bellini lived in Paris for the remainder of his short life, dying of an intestinal ailment on September 23, 1835.

Bellini is most known for his ten operas, though his output as a composer includes pieces for voice and piano. Most of his instrumental and sacred works were written prior to the premiere of his first opera in 1825, with the majority of his songs being written after 1825. While song was not what ultimately brought Bellini the greatest recognition, "Dolente immagine di Fille mia" was the first of his pieces to be published. It was written while Bellini was attending school in Naples. Bellini dedicated the song "to his friend Nicola Tauro." Bellini's compositional style is the epitome of pure, romantic Italian vocal melody, known as *bel canto* (beautiful singing).

Dolente immagine di Fille mia

Mournful image of my Fille

Dolente immagine di Fille mia,
Perchè sì squallida mi siedi accanto?
Che de più desideri?
Dirotto pianto
Io sul tuo cenere versai finor.
Temi che immemore de' sacri giuri
Io possa accendermi ad altra face?
Ombra di Fillide, riposa in pace;
È inestinguibile l'antico ardor.

Mournful image of my Fille,
Why are you so agonized next to me?
What more do you desire?
I have wept my eyes out
Onto your ashes up to now.
Do you fear that, forgetful of the sacred vows,
I could be ignited to another flame?
Spirit of Fillide, rest in peace;
Inextinguishable is our old passion.

Copyright © 2004 by HAL LEONARD CORPORATION
International Copyright Secured   All Rights Reserved

O del mio amato ben

Alberto Donaudy
(1880-1941)

Stefano Donaudy
(1879-1925)

Original key: A-flat major. Italian composer Stefano Donaudy was born in Palermo, on the island of Sicily, on February 21, 1879, and died in Naples on the mainland on May 30, 1925. Donaudy is remembered for his charming Italian songs. Stefano's talent surfaced early. His first opera, *Folchetto*, premiered in Palermo in 1892, when Donaudy was only 13 years old. Donaudy's other operas include *Scampagnata* (1898), *Theodor Körner* (1902), *Sperduti nel buio* (1907), *Ramuntcho* (1921), and *La Fiamminga* (1922). Donaudy's younger brother Alberto (1880-1941) collaborated with him on many projects, co-writing the libretto with Roberto Bracco for *Sperduti nel buio* and writing the libretto for *Theodor Körner*. This opera was based on the life of Körner, a German poet and revolutionary in the time of Napoleon. The Donaudy brothers followed numerous composers, most notably Franz Schubert, in their treatment of Körner's poems and life in music. Donaudy also composed a symphonic poem titled *Le Rêve*.

Most of Donaudy's output has been forgotten today, but his songs are still popular. First published by Ricordi in two volumes in 1918 and 1922 under the name *Arie di stille antico* (Arias in Antique Style), these 36 songs have texts written by Donaudy's brother Alberto. The term "antico" (antique) refers not to the period in which they were written, but rather to Donaudy's use of older song forms, like the arie, arietta, ballatella, canzone, canzonetta, frottola, madrigal, maggiolata, and villanella. These lushly romantic songs have been recorded by singers from Enrico Caruso to Andrea Bocelli.

O del mio amato ben

Oh of my dearly beloved…

O del mio amato ben perduto incanto!
Lungi è dagli occhi miei
chi m'era gloria e vanto!
Or per le mute stanze
sempre la (lo) cerco e chiamo
con pieno il cor di speranze…
Ma cerco invan, chiamo invan!
E il pianger m'è sì caro,
che di pianto sol nutro il cor.

Oh lost spell of my dearly beloved!
Far it is from my eyes
that which was my glory and virtue!
Now throughout the silent rooms
always I try to find her (him) and cry out
with my heart full of hopes…
But I search in vain, I call out in vain!
Crying is so beloved
that only by crying do I console my heart.

Mi sembra, senza lei (lui), triste ogni loco.
Notte mi sembra il giorno;
mi sembra gelo il foco.
Se pur talvolta spero
di darmi ad altra cura,
sol mi tormenta un pensiero:
ma, senza lei (lui), che farò?
Mi par così la vita vana cosa
senza il mio ben.

To me, it seems, without her (him) every place seems sad.
Night to me feels like day;
to me, ice seems like fire.
Sometimes I hope
to follow another direction,
I am tortured by one thought:
Without her (him), what will I do?
To me, life has no point
without my beloved.

Andante quasi adagio

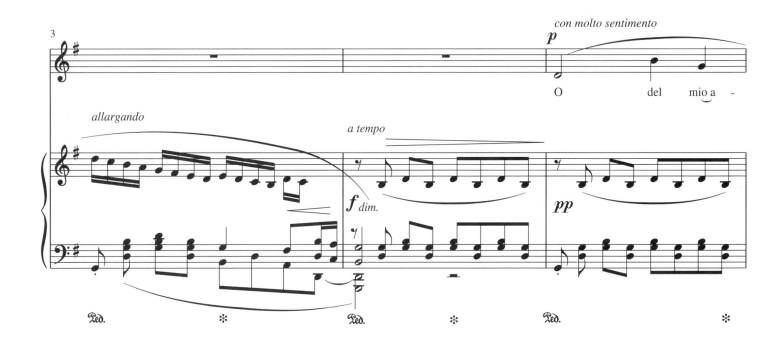

Se nel ben sempre incostante

Alessandro Stradella
(1644-1682)

Alessandro Stradella, a versatile composer of nearly every genre, led a colorful life of musical success, danger and intrigue. Born in Rome, both his parents died at an early age. It is not known who took care of him after their deaths, however. Stradella seems to have risen to a high social rank, living the carefree life afforded by his class. In 1669 he was banished from Rome for the first time after attempting to steal money from the Roman Catholic Church. He would return, only to be permanently banned from the city in 1677 after offending a Cardinal. He had many adventures with women. Stradella survived an attack by bandits after running away with the mistress of an important Venetian, and also an assassination attempt by those same men in 1677. The composer pursued a socially prominent Genoese woman, and as a result was killed at the Piazza Bianchi in Genoa. Stradella was an important musical presence in his time, and his music continued to be performed some years after his death. This aria is from one of the composer's many stage works. The realization/arrangement is by Alessandro Parisotti, who created the first modern edition of Italian Baroque songs for Ricordi in the 1880s. Parisotti's versions, though not authentic to Baroque performance practice, are historical in their own right, and capture the lyrical beauty of these songs.

Se nel ben sempre incostante

If in good times the always inconstant [fortune]

Se nel ben sempre incostante
Fortuna vagante
Di farsi stabile uso non ha,
Anco mutabile nel mal sarà.

If in good times the always inconstant
fortune, roaming,
is not used to making itself steady,
it will be volatile in bad times as well.

Realization/arrangement by Alessandro Parisotti

Cara e dolce

Anonymous

Alessandro Scarlatti
(1660-1725)

Alessandro Scarlatti is remembered especially for his operas and cantatas, and is often credited with being the founder of the Neapolitan school of 18th-century opera, though he may be more rightly credited as the last master of Venetian opera. As a child, Alessandro was sent to Rome with his two sisters. This was due to famine and turmoil in Palermo, but also to better immerse the young musician in a city full of culture. It was during these formative years that his musical style was developed. In Rome he would have heard the operas of Cesti, Cavalli, and Stradella. His earliest surviving vocal output was an oratorio commissioned in 1679. Later that same year his earliest known opera, *Gil equivoci nel sembiante*, was staged. After traveling around Italy and Germany, Scarlatti settled in Naples in the early 1680s. Naples at that point was not yet a famous musical and operatic city, but after the arrival of Scarlatti, its reputation quickly grew. Over the next 18 years, over half the new operas heard in the city were by Scarlatti. Most of these were *dramma per musica*, a well-defined type of opera with serious action and a happy ending. During those Naples years, Scarlatti composed 40 or so known operas, seven serenatas, nine oratorios, and 65 cantatas. We can assume that "Cara e dolce" is an operatic aria. Domenico Scarlatti (1685-1757), noted composer especially of keyboard sonatas, was the sixth of Alessandro Scarlatti's 10 children.

Cara e dolce	*Dear and sweet*
Cara e dolce, dolcissima libertà,	*Dear and sweet, sweetest freedom,*
Quanto ti piange il core;	*how much my heart weeps for you;*
Fra i lacci d'un crin d'oro	*among the ties of golden tresses*
Prova d'un ciglio arcier la crudeltà.	*it feels the cruelty of an arrow-hurling [Cupid's] brow.*
Cara e dolce, dolcissima libertà,	*Dear and sweet, sweetest freedom,*
Le dure ritorte che rigida sorte	*the harsh fetters which stern fate*
Mi da per mercé mi stringono il piè	*gives me as reward impede my way*
E al mio lungo penar negan pietà.	*and deny pity for my long suffering.*

La maja dolorosa

(número 2)

from *Colección de tonadillas*

Fernando Periquet
(1873-1940)

Enrique Granados
(1867-1916)

Enrique Granados was Catalan by birth. His family moved to Barcelona, where he began his musical studies. A scholarship allowed Granados to spend two years as an "auditeur" at the Paris Conservertoire. His first success as a composer came in Madrid with the premiere of his first opera, *María del Carmen*, in 1898. In 1909 Granados began work on the piano suite *Goyescas*, with which he achieved international recognition in 1914 after its Paris premiere. This piece was expanded into an opera, which was premiered at the Metropolitan Opera in New York in 1916. Its success resulted in an invitation for Granados to perform for President Wilson in Washington, D.C. On his trip back to Europe, the ship on which he returned was torpedoed in the English Channel. Granados was rescued but then drowned in a desperate and futile attempt to save his wife. Granados' music is rooted in a blend of Spanish nationalism, Spanish historical musical characteristics and European compositional tradition. His major contributions to vocal literature are the 12 *Tonadillas* of 1910-1911, inspired both by the theme of romantic love and etchings of Francisco Goya, though it is not a cycle in the true sense of the word.

La maja dolorosa número 2	*The sorrowful maja No. 2*
¡Ay majo de mi vida, no, no, tú no has muerto!	*Ay! Love of my life, no, no, you have not died!*
¿Acaso yo existiese si fuera eso cierto?	*How could I exist if this were true?*
¡Quiero loca besar tu boca!	*I want crazily to kiss your mouth!*
Quiero segura, gozar más de tu ventura.	*I want safely to enjoy more of your happiness.*
¡Ay! de tu ventura!	*Ay! of your happiness!*
Mas, ¡ay! deliro, sueño: mi majo no existe.	*But ay, I rave, dream, my lover doesn't exist.*
En torno mío el mundo lloroso está y triste.	*Around me the world is sobbing and sad.*
¡A mí duelo no hallo consuelo!	*In my mourning I do not find comfort.*
Mas muerto y frío	*But dead and cold*
siempre el majo será mío. ¡Ay! Siempre mío.	*always the lover will be mine. Ay! Always mine.*

Andantino con dolore

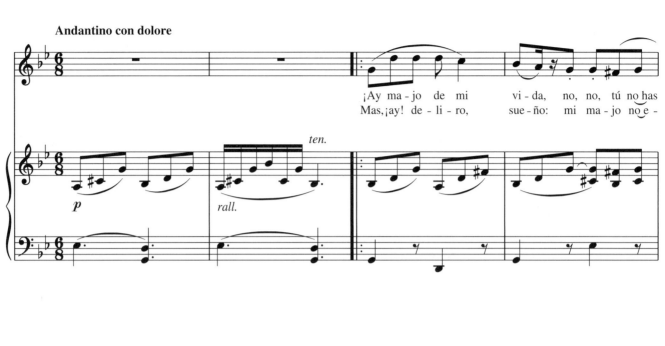

¡Ay ma - jo de mi vi - da, no, no, tú no has
Mas, ¡ay! de - li - ro, sue - ño: mi ma - jo no e -

muer - to! ____ ¿A - ca - so yo e - xis - tie - se si fue - ra e - so cier - to? ____ ¡Quie - ro
xis - te. ____ En tor - no mí - o el mun - do llo - ro - so es - tá y tris - te. ____ ¡A mí

lo - ca be - sar ___ tu bo - ca! ____ Quie - ro, se - gu - ra, go - zar más de tu ven -
due - lo no ha - llo con - sue - lo! ____ Mas muer - to y frí - o siem - pre el ma - jo se - rá

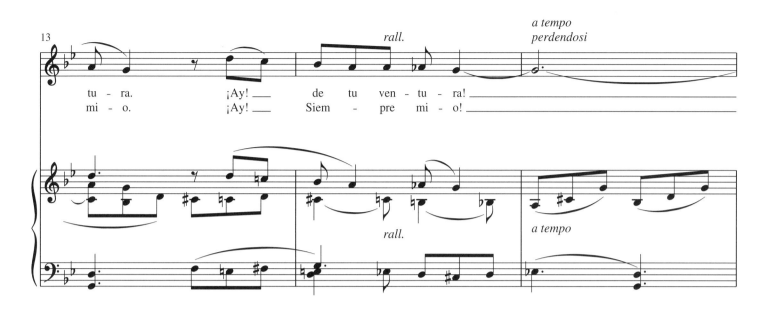

tu - ra.   ¡Ay!___ de tu ven - tu - ra!___

mi - o.   ¡Ay!___ Siem - pre mi - o!___

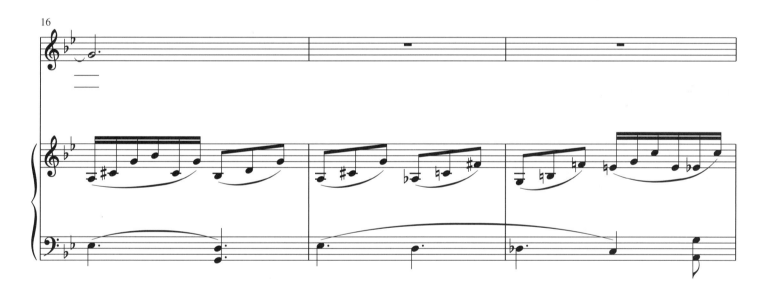

El paño moruno

from *Siete canciones populares españolas*

Spanish Folk Poetry

Manuel de Falla
(1876-1946)

Manuel de Falla was able to meld the essence of the Spanish folksong with early 20th-century French and Spanish compositional techniques. His formative years of musical training and composition in Spain culminated in 1905 when the Real Academia de Belles Artes de San Fernando sponsored a contest for a Spanish opera, which Falla won with *La vida breve* (The Brief Life). In 1907 he went to France for a seven day concert tour and stayed seven years. His exposure to impressionism in music proved to be the greatest influence on him as a composer. In Paris he was introduced to Ravel, Stravinsky, Debussy, and Dukas as well as other important figures of the cultural life of that city. *Siete canciones populares españolas* (Seven Popular Spanish Songs) was completed in 1914 while Falla was still in Paris. He based these songs on Spanish folk material representing the various regions of the country. The accompaniments are pianistic, containing modal sonorities and creative treatment of the original melodic material. The *Siete canciones* have found a place in the standard repertoire internationally and have been orchestrated.

El paño moruno	*The moorish cloth*
Al paño fino, en la tienda,	*On the fine cloth, in the store*
Al paño fino, en la tienda,	*On the fine cloth, in the store*
Una mancha le cayó;	*A stain set it*
Una mancha le cayó;	*A stain set in*
Por menos precio se vende,	*For a lower price it is sold*
Por menos precio se vende,	*For a lower price it is sold*
Porque perdió su valor.	*Because it has lost its value*
Porque perdió su valor.	*Because it has lost its value*
¡Ay!	*Oh!*

Allegretto vivace (♩. = 72)

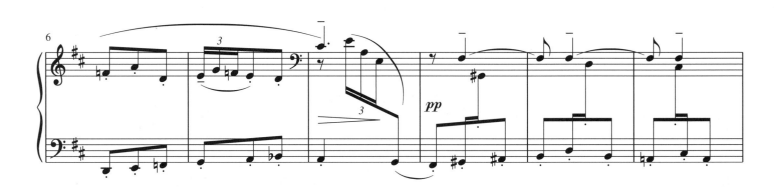

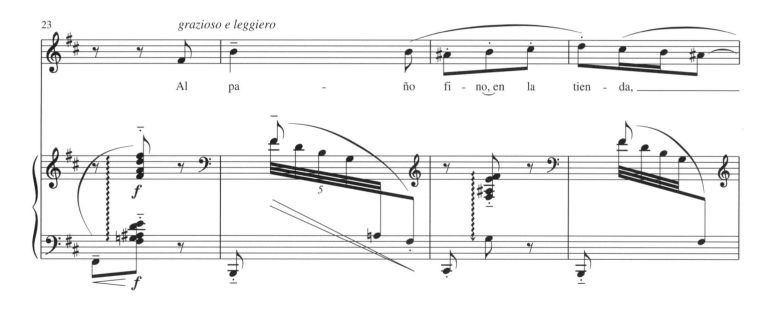

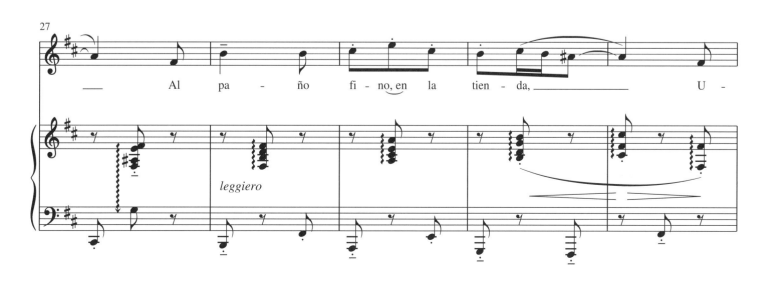

Voi che sapete
from
LE NOZZE DI FIGARO

libretto by
Lorenzo Da Ponte
(1749-1838)

Wolfgang Amadeus Mozart
(1756-1791)

Le nozze di Figaro was first performed in Vienna at the Burgtheater on May 1, 1786. The libretto, written by Lorenzo Da Ponte, was based on *La Folle Journée, ou Le Mariage de Figaro*, a comedy by Augustin Caron de Beaumarchais. The original Beaumarchais play was banned in Vienna, due to its political content. The play is the sequel to *Le barbier de Séville*, which enjoyed success in Giovanni Paisiello's operatic version, and is most well known in Gioachino Rossini's version. Mozart finished the opera on April 29, 1786, two days before its premiere. The opera was fairly well received in Vienna, receiving nine performances, and was revived in 1789 and 1790, receiving 26 further performances. At the end of 1786, Mozart traveled to Prague to conduct *Figaro*, where it had previously achieved tremendous success. This trip eventually led to the commission of *Don Giovanni*, which had its world premiere in Prague.

The opera takes place at the palace of Count Almavira near Seville, and is about the various struggles in the relationships of those in the court, including the servants. Cherubino is a page to the Count. The pubescent boy has boundless energy and is in a fever for all women. The Count finds Cherubino a nuisance one too many times, and sends him off to the army. The boy is crushed, and goes to the Countess and Susanna to tell them his fate. Susanna asks him to sing one of his love songs, and he performs "Voi che sapete" for the two ladies.

Voi che sapete che cosa è amor,	*You know what love is,*
donne vedete s'io l'ho nel cor.	*tell me if it's in my heart.*
Quello ch'io provo, vi ridirò,	*What I feel, I'll explain to you,*
è per me nuovo, capir nol so.	*It's new to me, I can't comprehend.*
Sento un affetto pien di desir,	*I feel an emotion charged with desire,*
ch'ora è diletto, ch'ora è martir;	*which is first delight, then torture.*
Gelo, e poi sento l'alma avvampar,	*I freeze, then I feel my soul burst into flame,*
e in un momento torno a gelar.	*in a moment I am frozen again.*
Ricerco un bene fuori di me:	*I search for a treasure that is not within me.*
non so chi il tiene, non so cos'è;	*I don't know who holds it, or where it is;*
sospiro e gemo senza voler,	*I sigh and moan though I don't want to,*
palpito e tremo senza saper;	*my heart races and trembles, and I know not why;*
Non trovo pace notte nè dì,	*I find peace neither night nor day,*
ma pur mi piace languir così.	*yet I like to languish like this.*

CHERUBINO:

Voi, che sa - pe - te che co - sa è a - mor,

don - ne, ve - de - te, s'io l'ho nel cor,

don - ne, ve - de - te,____ s'io l'ho__ nel__ cor.

Quel - lo ch'io pro - vo, vi____ ri - di - rò;____

è per me nuo - vo, ca - pir nol so.

Sen - to un af - fet - to pien di de - sir,____

che co - sa è a - mor, don - ne, ve - de - te

s'io l'ho nel cor, don - ne, ve - de - te,____

s'io l'ho nel cor, don - ne, ve - de - te,____

s'io l'ho____ nel____ cor.

Che farò senza Euridice?
from
ORFEO ED EURIDICE

libretto by
Raniero de Calzabigi
(1714-1795)

Christoph Wilibald Gluck
(1714-1784)

German composer Christoph Willibald Gluck is remembered most as the composer who reformed opera, moving it away from the highly stylized *opera seria* to a more expressive and dramatic art form. Gluck did not receive the musical education of most composers of his stature. His father was a forester and never supported his son's musical growth. Determined to succeed, Christoph ran away to Prague at age 13 or 14, and continued to travel around Europe until settling in Vienna around 1752. He was primarily self-taught, which gave him a simple style, devoid of complicated counterpoint. Operas to this point were very strict in their form. They relied on rigid alternation between recitative and aria, formal librettos, and florid, and often excessive, vocal displays. Gluck wrote 29 operas in this old style, but this all changed in 1762 with *Orfeo ed Euridice*. Premiering in Vienna on October 5, the emperor's name day, *Orfeo* was a resounding success. The libretto by Raniero Calzabigi owed much to *opera seria* and its conventions, but the work was unified by an overall structure that accentuated larger themes of nobility and truth of feeling. Gluck's elegant melodies were simple and unadorned, allowing for a clarity of lyric and emotional directness lacking in *opera seria*. His alternation between recitative and aria was not strict, instead it was used freely to serve the drama.

This opera is based on Greek myth. Orfeo (Orpheus), the most able musician, descends into the underworld, the realm of the dead. Through his songs he persuades the guards at the gates of Hades to allow him to find his beloved Euridice there. They agree, but if Orfeo looks at her before they leave Hades, she will die and remain there. Euridice pleads with Orfeo for a look and will not follow him without it. He reluctantly gives her a glance, and Euridice dies. The aria is Orfeo's lament. This is a "pants role," meaning a woman singer portraying a male character, a convention in opera.

Ahimè! Dove trascorsi?	*Alas! Where have I passed?*
Dove mi spinse un delirio d'amor?	*Where has a delirium of love thrust me?*
Sposa! Euridice! Consorte!	*Bride! Euridice! Wife!*
Ah, più non vive! La chiamo in van.	*Ah, she lives no more; I call her to no avail.*
Misero me, la perdo	*Poor me – She's gone,*
e di nuovo e per sempre!	*Now and for always!*
O legge! Oh morte!	*Oh law! Oh death!*
Oh ricordo crudel!	*Oh cruel recollection!*
Non ho soccorso,	*I do not have aid;*
non m'avanza consiglio	*for me there is no counsel!*
Io veggo solo	*I only*
(oh fiera vista!)	*(oh savage sight)*
il luttuoso aspetto	*the mournful appearance*
dell'orrido mio stato.	*of my horrible state.*
Saziati, sorte rea:	*Be satiated, cruel fate:*
son disperato!	*I am without hope!*
Che farò senza Euridice?	*What will I do without Euridice?*
Dove andrò senza il mio ben?	*Where will I go without my beloved?*
Che farò? Dove andrò?	*What will I do? Where will I go?*
Che farò senza il mio ben?	*What will I do without my beloved?*
Euridice! Oh Dio! Rispondi!	*Euridice! Oh God! Answer!*
Io son pure il tuo fedele.	*I am still faithful to you.*
Ah! non m'avanza più soccorso,	*Ah, no more aid*
più speranza	*nor hope comes to me*
nè dal mondo, nè dal ciel!	*from earth, or heaven!*

*Appoggiatura recommended

chia - mo in - van. Mi - se - ro

me, la per - do e di nuo - vo e per sem - pre! Oh leg - ge! Oh mor - te! Oh ri -

cor - do cru - del! Non ho soc - cor - so, non m'a - van - za con - si - glio Io veg-go so - lo (Oh

— fie - ra vi - sta!) il lut - tu - o - so a - spet - to dell' or - ri - do mio sta - to!

William Schwenck Gilbert
Arthur Seymour Sullivan

The names Gilbert and Sullivan are not only synonymous with operetta, they are nearly inseparable one from the other. The 14 operettas the pair produced, virtually the only English operettas of the era that have survived, are the principal works by which the two are remembered, despite the fact that both men had extensive careers apart from their partnership. The appeal of the operettas was due to equally important contributions from Gilbert and Sullivan. Gilbert, for his part, created librettos that mixed fantastical, ridiculous plots populated by comically flawed characters, with critical commentaries on the foibles and failings of British society and government. Sullivan held up his end of the partnership by providing remarkably balanced, irrepressible melodies that softened the impact of Gilbert's social criticisms, and at the same time, highlighted them. As individuals, Gilbert and Sullivan were as different as their respective contributions to the partnership.

Sir William Schwenck Gilbert, knighted in 1907 and acknowledged as one of the great English literary figures of his age, was an upright, proper gentleman, almost rigid in character. For all his personal pomposity, his greatest delight was in things ridiculous. His views on the silly side of life are best expressed by a line he gave to the character Jack Point in *The Yeomen of the Guard*: "…there is humour in all things, and the truest philosophy is that which teaches us to find it and make the most of it." Gilbert loved to create worlds in which characters and situations were the opposite of what they seemed, a realm he referred to as Topsy-Turvydom. His delight in creating a topsy-turvy world is evident in stories or situations Gilbert created in his *Bab Ballads*, poems dubbed with his childhood nickname to give them a catchy title. He illustrated these works with drawings, as he later would illustrate his librettos, which also echo the *Bab Ballads*. Gilbert's childhood surfaced in one of the vehicles he used for these crazy twists of plot as well, as he himself was kidnapped from the care of a nanny at age two while his family was traveling in Naples. He was returned after a ransom was paid. The incident, perhaps combined with a cold, unhappy home life that ended with his parents parting company when Gilbert was 19, raised the nagging question of how life might have been different had he been raised by someone else.

Sir Arthur Seymour Sullivan, knighted in 1883, wanted to be respected and remembered for his "serious" works. His musical talent was recognized at an early age, his music first appearing in print when he was 13. Arthur won large scholarships in his teens that allowed him to study in Leipzig for several years. Although apparently an agnostic, he took several positions as a church organist, and composed quite a few hymns, including "Onward Christian Soldiers" and the standard British setting of "It Came upon a Midnight Clear" (a different tune from its American counterpart). But Sullivan's serious music was largely thought to be too weighty and ponderous, and even a bit stilted. Among Sullivan's most important contributions to "serious" music are the discoveries he made, with Sir George Grove, of two lost symphonies by Franz Schubert, as well as finding Schubert's incidental music for the play *Rosamunde*. Sullivan's gift for melody found its freest expression in the operetta genre. Where Gilbert was upright and uptight, Sullivan was a libertarian. Gilbert was tall and fair-haired; Sullivan was short, dark-haired and fairly round. He was fond of the physical pleasures of life, smoking heavily, drinking and eating with abandon. Gilbert was a devoted, proper husband; Sullivan never married, choosing instead to indulge in frequent amorous encounters. He spent his last 20 years with Mrs. Mary Frances Reynolds, an American estranged from her husband.

When Frederic Was a Little Lad
from *The Pirates of Penzance*

The London premiere was at the Opéra Comique on April 3, 1880. Pirate festivities on the Cornwall coast open this satire on British military and constabulary, celebrating the completion of young Frederic's pirate internship. His situation is explained by Ruth, his nursemaid, in **"When Frederic Was a Little Lad."** Apparently she mistook Frederic's father's instruction to apprentice him as a pilot and instead set him up as a pirate. Frederic must, for duty's sake, return to the honest world and work to end piracy thereby betraying his pirate friends. Just then, a party of young maidens appear, and are shocked to find a pirate in their midst. Frederic pleads for a maiden to take pity on him. Mabel appears and bravely offers him her heart. The pirates spot the maidens and creep in to kidnap them. The girls' father, the Major-General appears, hoping to foil the pirates' plans of marriage. He knows that the pirates are orphans and are tenderhearted toward other orphans, explaining that he too is an orphan and would be lost without his daughters. The pirates relent and the Major-General, Frederic and the girls depart, leaving Ruth with the pirates. The Major-General confesses to Frederic and Mabel that he is not an orphan. Frederic explains his plans to put the pirates out of business, and is in the process of proposing to Mabel when policemen arrive on their way to conquer the pirates themselves. The Pirate King and Ruth arrive with a most ingenious paradox. Frederic was born on a leap-year day, so he won't actually reach his 21st birthday until 1940. Therefore he is still the pirates' apprentice. A slave to duty, Frederic returns to his pirate life, where honor forces him to tell the pirates that the Major-General is not an orphan. The policemen prepare to arrest the pirates, who in turn are sneaking up on the Major-General. The policemen are defeated almost immediately. The police are about to be killed until they pull Union Jacks from their pockets and command the pirates to stand down in the name of Queen Victoria. The pirates, who love their Queen, comply. Ruth puts everything to rights by explaining that the pirates are actually noblemen who have gone wrong. They are immediately forgiven and given back their titles. Frederic and Mabel reunite and the Major-General asks the pirates/nobles to marry his daughters.

When Frederic Was a Little Lad

from

THE PIRATES OF PENZANCE

W.S. Gilbert
(1836-1911)

Arthur Sullivan
(1842-1900)

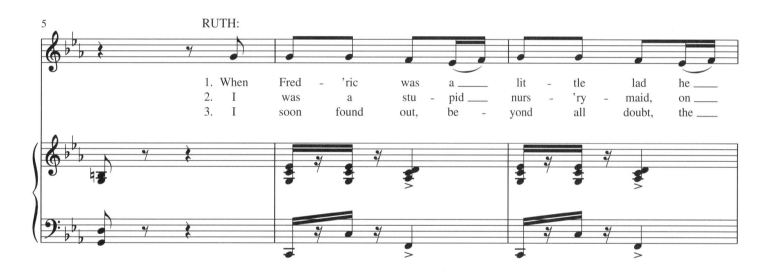

23

har - dy lad, though _ sure - ly not a high lot, Though
was to make, and _ doom him to a vile lot, I
find me now, a _ mem - ber of your shy lot, Which you

26

I'm a nurse, you might do worse than make your boy a
bound him to a pi - rate— you!— in - stead of to a a
would - n't have found, had he been bound ap - pren - tice to a

29

1, 2

pi - lot!
pi - lot!

3

pi - lot!

f   *f*

32

Antonio Vivaldi

Italian composer Antonio Vivaldi was one of the most original and influential Italian composers of his generation. Very prolific, he claimed to be able to write a concerto faster than a copyist could prepare the parts. He wrote around 500 concertos and sinfonias, 90 solo and trio sonatas, 49 operas, and many cantatas, motets, and oratorios. The composer's strong personality and style, as well as his enormous output, make him the major late Baroque Italian figure in music history. Put simply, Bach, Handel and Vivaldi are the essence of music of the period.

Antonio trained to be a priest as a youth, but continued to live at home, allowing ample time to study music and take lessons from his father, a violinist at St. Mark's in Venice. Vivaldi was ordained as a priest in 1703, though he stopped giving mass shortly afterwards. Because of his red hair he was often called "il prete rosso," the redheaded priest. His first official post was *maestro di violino* at Pio Ospedale della Pietà, where he taught music lessons to the orphaned girl residents. He held this position off and on from 1703 until 1740. Vivaldi conducted the students in concerts that were very well attended by locals and travelers.

Qui sedes ad dexteram Patris
from *Gloria*

Vivaldi's sacred vocal music is heavily influenced by opera; his cantatas and serenatas exhibit standard *da capo* aria form, broken up by passages of recitative. These sacred works were all written for church festivals and services. His *Gloria*, RV 589, is the second of two D major Glorias composed by Vivaldi. The text is the traditional Gloria section from the Latin Mass of the Roman Catholic liturgy. No exact chronology of Vivaldi's sacred works exists, but both Glorias are believed to have been written after 1708. In general, Vivaldi's music fell out of the repertory until the mid-20th century. The first modern performance of this Gloria took place in Siena, Italy, in 1939, and the piece quickly became one of the most performed large sacred choral works.

Qui sedes ad dexteram patris,	*Who sits on the right hand of the Father*
Misrere nobis.	*have mercy on us.*

Qui sedes ad dexteram Patris

from
GLORIA

Antonio Vivaldi
(1678-1741)